Praise for
What Is God Waiting For?

There are some books that offer impressive technical advice but lack
real-life application. There are other books with nuggets of wisdom that
can be immediately put into practice because they have been birthed in the
crucible of life. *What Is God Waiting For?* fits into the latter category.
I have watched my wife, Marlinda, live the principles in this book.
Now she offers you a wonderful opportunity to be strengthened by
the truths she's learned during her seasons of divine delays.

DAVID D. IRELAND, PH.D.
SENIOR PASTOR, CHRIST CHURCH, MONTCLAIR, NEW JERSEY
AUTHOR, *PERFECTING YOUR PURPOSE* AND *THE SECRETS OF A SATISFYING LIFE*

Marlinda Ireland is very explicit about the fact that we can wait on God and
still see God work the miracles in our lives for which we are believing. We
don't praise Him *when* the answer comes; we praise Him *until* the answer
comes. This book will give you courage and hope to keep believin'.

JUDY JACOBS
AUTHOR, PSALMIST AND SPEAKER
HIS SONG MINISTRIES, CLEVELAND, OHIO

What Is God Waiting For? parts company with typical self-help books,
as it brings principles from God's Word in addition to a real challenge
to our earthbound mind-sets. It first defines and explains the source
of delays, then it releases us to explore new possibilities during the
postponement phase of God's ultimate will in our lives. The answers
Marlinda Ireland has learned may surprise you—making the wait
not only bearable but also exciting. This book is a must-read for those
who feel that they are in a holding pattern in God's purposes.

HARRY AND MICHELE JACKSON
PASTORS OF HOPE CHRISTIAN CHURCH
COLLEGE PARK, MARYLAND

In this "microwave" society, delay is considered unacceptable. Marlinda Ireland makes a strong point to remind us that God's "delay is not denial." Each time she uses the phrase, it's with an eye on the promise of coming fulfillment. Through personal experience and examples from the lives of Bible characters, Marlinda instills hope and faith in us to rise above discouragement when we are on God's detours. Even in the prison of our circumstances, God is working a greater purpose. In this work, the maturing Christian has a true manual for embracing the bigger picture despite the crisis of the moment.

REVEREND PAUL JOHANSSON
PRESIDENT, ELIM BIBLE INSTITUTE

Every so often a book comes along that expresses the heart of God for the times. *What Is God Waiting For?* is a book for this season in which God is calling us to begin a journey toward our promise. Many of us have been waiting a long time to experience the blessings that God revealed were ours. Marlinda's book shows us the power in waiting. She has an incredible ability to integrate biblical characters who waited for their promise into a modern reality to which any reader can relate. In a world in which we could fear the future, this book reveals that the blessings of life are worth waiting for.

CHUCK D. PIERCE
PRESIDENT, GLORY OF ZION INTERNATIONAL MINISTRIES, INC.
VICE PRESIDENT, GLOBAL HARVEST MINISTRIES

There's nothing worse than feeling like a faithless, second-class Christian while waiting on the promises of God. But every now and then, a book breaks away from the pack and reaches right into your soul! Pastor Marlinda takes the mystery and the misconception out of the pathway of finding your destiny. This book will help you to endure *the pain of the process of life* and connect you with the *missing link* in renewing your hope and your trust in God.

ALVIN SLAUGHTER
FOUNDER AND PRESIDENT,
ALVIN SLAUGHTER CONCERTS
FAITH LIFE INTERNATIONAL

In a time when many people are trying to hear God's voice above their own, I believe the principles in this book provide the answers that many seek. *What Is God Waiting For?* will cause many to rest in God, confident that "if He said it He will do it," while others will be challenged to reposition themselves and begin to stamp out delays caused by their own actions and wills. Marlinda, you are an example of the new thing God is doing in the marketplace. You go, girl!

GLORIA SLAUGHTER
PRESIDENT, GLORIA INTERNATIONAL
WOMEN OF POWER AND PRAYER

What is
God Waiting for?

MARLINDA IRELAND

Regal

From Gospel Light
Ventura, California, U.S.A.

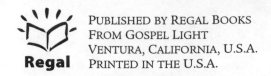

PUBLISHED BY REGAL BOOKS
FROM GOSPEL LIGHT
VENTURA, CALIFORNIA, U.S.A.
PRINTED IN THE U.S.A.

Regal Books is a ministry of Gospel Light, a Christian publisher dedicated to serving the local church. We believe God's vision for Gospel Light is to provide church leaders with biblical, user-friendly materials that will help them evangelize, disciple and minister to children, youth and families.

It is our prayer that this Regal book will help you discover biblical truth for your own life and help you meet the needs of others. May God richly bless you.

For a free catalog of resources from Regal Books/Gospel Light, please call your Christian supplier or contact us at 1-800-4-GOSPEL or www.regalbooks.com.

Library of Congress Cataloging-in-Publication Data
Ireland, Marlinda.
  What is God waiting for? / Marlinda Ireland.
    p. cm.
  ISBN 0-8307-3911-4 (trade paper)
  1. Providence and government of God. 2. Expectation (Psychology)—Religious aspects—Christianity. 3. Trust in God. 4. Waiting (Philosophy) 5. Patience—Religious aspects—Christianity. I. Title.
  BT135.I74 2006
  231'.5—dc22   2006014087

1   2   3   4   5   6   7   8   9   10   /   10   09   08   07   06

Rights for publishing this book in other languages are contracted by Gospel Light Worldwide, the international nonprofit ministry of Gospel Light. Gospel Light Worldwide also provides publishing and technical assistance to international publishers dedicated to producing Sunday School and Vacation Bible School curricula and books in the languages of the world. For additional information, visit www.gospellightworldwide.org; write to Gospel Light Worldwide, P.O. Box 3875, Ventura, CA 93006; or send an e-mail to info@gospellightworldwide.org.

DEDICATION

This book is lovingly dedicated to my parents, Maceo and Mary Reaves, who taught me the power of waiting for God. Through the years, their constant support has been a tremendous source of encouragement. Their spirituality, generosity, integrity and patience have modeled stalwart devotion to God. I am forever indebted to them for being my first mentors in the art of waiting well.

Contents

Acknowledgments

People often ask me how I am able to accomplish so much in life. I believe the best answer to that question is summed up by the words, "When you see me—you see *we*." I could never do anything without the help of my family, friends, staff and supporters. I want to extend my personal and sincere thanks to:

My husband, David—a man of great strength and wisdom. Your love, support, advice and encouragement during the writing of this book made a challenging task much easier. God used you in more ways than you'll ever know. I am blessed to have you as my partner in life.

Danielle and Jessica—my daughters, two best friends and satellites. You are beautiful inside and out. Your smiles and hugs always embolden and enrich me. Being your mother is my most treasured title.

Debbie DiPasquale—your prayers, encouragement, timely insights and dedication are priceless. I still don't know how you held down the fort in the office while I worked to complete this project. You have helped me accomplish so many of my assignments from God. May God do for you what you have unselfishly done for me.

Lee Hough—without your tenacity, this project would not have come to fruition. Thanks for sticking with me.

Kim Bangs—words cannot express my appreciation for you and the folks at Regal. Thanks for believing in the message of this book and in me.

Cinda Gaskin—for sprinkling your fairy dust on the pages of this manuscript.

The People of Christ Church—for your love, prayers, dedication and enthusiasm. In many ways, your lives acted as a canvas for this project. You are my joy.

Prologue

When I sat down to write this book, I had no idea that it would forever transform *my* perspective of life. I believed that during the past 20 years I'd had a pretty good dose of waiting for God. So I began this project with the intent to help others who struggle with God's timing for their lives. Yet by the time I had put the last period on the last sentence, *I* felt a brand-new degree of freedom. It was as though my own struggle had come to a close. God used the writing of this book to help me embrace some of the more subtle nudgings of the Holy Spirit that I had overlooked or forgotten. These were delicate dealings that I had somehow taken for granted along the way. God taught me the deeper meaning of waiting for Him.

It would be safe to say that we are all waiting for God to do *something* for us. Parents are waiting for wayward children; the lonely are waiting for the love of their lives; the sick are waiting to be healed; the unemployed and underemployed are waiting for their needs to be met. We all hunger to experience a promise fulfilled or a prayer answered. We are all thirsty for tomorrow.

I'm sure that your wait has been longer than you ever thought it would be. If you're like me, you've already done everything you know to do in order to position yourself for a breakthrough. Yet the promise has not come. Why? Over the years, I have found that this road of waiting for God has one significant lesson to teach but many secrets to tell. What is the lesson? It's that the future belongs to God. He alone owns and oversees it. Most of us sense this truth, but we also deny it.

I have also found that this challenging path does not easily let go of its precious secrets. What are they? These are the secrets you'll discover as you journey with me through this book, taking a backward look into history and reaching forward to somehow seize a deeper understanding of the unfathomable God. Once these secrets are grasped, you'll have to fight to retain what you hear. You'll have to wrestle to overcome the diseases that waiting brings. And you'll have to struggle to maintain your balance on the tightrope of delay, because—contrary to popular opinion—time and God never stand still.

Most of us know that we live in a microwave millennium where everything happens at a fast and furious pace. This lifestyle and its accompanying mentality have caused many to ask, "Why does it take God so long to answer my most urgent prayers?" This painful and perplexing issue lurks in the dark corners of our minds, often hindering us from surviving the unexplained delays we face in life. These kinds of questions fly in the face of our faith—especially when our priorities, planning, perspectives and prayers are all on target. What should you do when you've completed the checklist of prerequisites to answered prayer and there is still no victory in sight? What do you do when time is no longer your friend and hope has all but dried up? What do you do when you are facing a divine delay?

The answers to these questions lie in the biblical stories of men and women who persevered in waiting for God. *What Is God Waiting For?* focuses on numerous biblical accounts of bona fide instances of divine delays. Without fail, each intermission of human history by God is a glorious thing and holds a purpose and an enduring lesson for today's believer. In this book, I'll show how biblical characters and others successfully made it to their desired end with their faith *and* their future intact. The resulting survival secrets are presented in a practical manner—one that strengthens your perspective of God. You'll grow in your ability to trust that the delay will work a God-inspired and meaningful ending to your challenge. Through step-by-step application of sound biblical principles, you'll be propelled out of the disappointment of your divine delay and into a renewed passion for God's perspective about your future.

Yet I will not insult your intelligence or your spirituality with promises of an immediate transition from a divine delay into an instant delight. Don't expect magical formulas or catchy incantations. This book is for those who have tried in futility all of the fad faith methods for getting God to do what only He can do, but who eventually learned that God does not perform for anyone. This book is for those tired, disappointed but spiritually hungry people who have come to the conclusion, "There must be a deeper revelation of why God waits."

I hope to take you on a journey of discovery in which you'll begin to understand the heart of God regarding His sovereign timing in your life. It is my prayer that you'll find life lessons to ultimately change your perspective and ease your frustrations. May these truths transform your life as you continue to wait for God.

CHAPTER ONE

The Wrong Thing at the Right Time

EXPERIENCE IS WHAT YOU GET WHEN YOU DON'T GET WHAT YOU WANT.

One of the greatest challenges we face in life is that of mistaking our timing for God's timing. Many years ago, I learned about this the hard way. Growing up in a close-knit family didn't prepare me for the independent life of a college student living on campus. Instead, my early college days were filled with a deep sense of isolation. This was the kind of loneliness that caused my bones to ache; the kind that caused me to soak my pillow with tears most nights.

One day, a close friend introduced me to Tom, a young man who was studying to become a lawyer at a nearby university. Tom was everything that I wanted in a man and then some. Not only was he a Christian, but he also was tall and handsome. He was kind and considerate, smart and—best of all—he was available! I hoped that Tom would treat me like the queen every little girl dreams of becoming—and he did. Soon after we began dating, my feelings for Tom blossomed. Yet despite the beautiful roses he brought me and the dates he took me on to some of the finest restaurants in town, I began to sense that something wasn't quite right.

After praying for direction, I felt that the Lord wanted me to end this seemingly storybook relationship. Initially, I ignored the feeling and prayed again about my misgivings. But the uneasiness continued. Stubbornly, I went on ignoring God's subtle warnings, thinking that I knew what was best for me.

As the relationship progressed, Tom began pressuring me about becoming intimate with him. I struggled with the thought, fearing the prospect of lapsing back into that ugly state of loneliness. I knew within my heart of hearts that I had to make a decision. I knew that while Tom had confessed Christ as Savior, his conduct and desires were saying something very different about his commitment in this area. And since I was still learning how to understand God's will for my life, I couldn't tell that his charm was merely an act—one intended to beguile me away from a serious walk with the Lord. I was overwhelmed with confusion.

One day, while Tom and I were talking, laughing and having a great time together, he stunned me with the announcement that he was going to find someone who really wanted to "be with him." It was as if I had blinked and the relationship was suddenly over. Tom had dropped me like a hot potato. I was so devastated by what I recognize now as this divine delay of my happiness that I cried for days.

Later, I realized that the relationship would never have worked. There were major differences in the critical areas of our relationship; namely, in our beliefs, values, and worldviews. In time, I came to see that God divinely intervened and kept me from deeper hurt and future frustration with Tom.

The lesson here is that it doesn't matter if it's Tommy, Tina, Tony or Tammy; the wrong thing at what may seem to be the right time is still the wrong thing. It doesn't matter if it is a job paying $150,000 a year or if it's the opportunity of a lifetime; the right thing at the wrong time is less than God's best. You must learn that being divinely delayed does not mean being denied.

I would love to tell you that my prince charming came along within a few days. But the fact of the matter is that my husband to be, David Ireland, did not come along until a few *years* later. Yet this divine delay taught me how to work through my feelings of loneliness by learning to enjoy my singleness. When I met David, there was no internal struggle. He was "the One," and I knew it. Now, after 22 years of marriage and 2 children, I can look back and thank God for His divine delay in the romantic area of my life.

WHY GOD'S DELAYS ARE DIVINE

In my temptation to continue my relationship with Tom, I wondered in frustration whether God would ever respond to my need for lasting companionship. The prophet Isaiah knew the answer when he said, "Therefore will the Lord wait, that he may be gracious to you" (Isa. 30:18, *KJV*). God was waiting to bring me a gracious gift. Since that time, I have learned that God's delays are divine and delightful because, in the end, we will experience the pleasure of a promise fulfilled. While I was with Tom, my desire for him was ripe, but my ability to discern God's will for my life was rotten.

Have you ever been tempted to act but somehow knew that you should wait? Have you ever thought that the timing was right for a particular decision, only to later discover that you had talked yourself into deception? God wants you to experience the power of receiving the *right* thing at the *right* time. God plans to send answers in response to your prayers, but waiting for Him is not always easy. Let's face it: Waiting is tough. Waiting is frustrating. And, if we're honest with ourselves, we can all agree that waiting stinks!

Waiting is especially hard in our microwave millennium. We are often judged by how quickly we reach the proverbial brass ring. If we are not happily married with two children, making a six-figure income, living in a five-bedroom house and enjoying all the finer things in life by age 35, we're labeled as someone who's behind schedule. Questions from well-meaning friends and family members can also make us feel inferior to people who have seemingly "arrived." We all have someone in our lives who is bold enough to ask, "So, when are you getting married?" or "Don't you want to have children?" or, worse, "Isn't it time for you to get a job that pays real money?"

In reality, most of us judge our insides by other people's outsides. The pressure to conform to unwritten timelines set by society is intense. However, comparing ourselves to others only leads to jealousy, envy, competition and discouragement. There comes a time when we must leave the driving of our dream to God. He has established a unique timeline for our life. Our lives are similar to fruit-bearing trees; different kinds of fruit ripen and mature at different seasons. Similarly, we each have a timetable wherein we blossom and ripen into the purposes of God. The Bible declares, "He has made everything beautiful in its time" (Eccles. 3:11, *AMP*). The rate at which our life's purpose is achieved is not always determined by our own efforts or schedules; it is also based on God's divine timing.

PICTURES FROM THE PAST

Throughout history, the Lord has used divine delays to bring His people to their ultimate purpose. A divine delay occurs when God postpones answering a prayer, even though the person posing the request is in right standing with Him. This delay is orchestrated and ordained by God.

Yes, it is a slow route to our destination. Yes, it is a rocky route. And yes, there is not much we can do to speed up the process. But divine delays are not denials. And they are not necessarily caused by human error, by lack of faith, or by disobedience. Divine delays occur when the desire of a person's heart is being withheld for a period of time and when that desire will only be released at God's appointed time. If, through no fault of your own, you are experiencing unexpected setbacks, unplanned hindrances, and unanswered prayers, you may be in a season of divine delay.

God provides powerful pictures of divine delays in Scripture. For example, God promised Abraham a son. But it was 25 years before Isaac was born to Abraham and his wife, Sarah. God also promised to give Abraham land for his inheritance. Yet that promise was not fulfilled for another 400 years. Further, God promised Moses a Savior, but Jesus did not appear until about 1,200 years later. Through Jesus Christ, God promised the gift of the Holy Spirit to His Church, and the disciples were told to go to the upper room and wait. Fifty days after Jesus ascended into heaven, on the Day of Pentecost, the promised Holy Spirit came on the scene.

These are only a few of the many pictures of God's divine delays. In each delay, there is a powerful story depicting God's genius at work. His track record proves that delays are not denials. God's design also shows that our lives are intricately

WE ARE NOT PAWNS, BUT VITAL PLAYERS ON GOD'S TEAM.
WHEN HE NEEDS US IN THE LINEUP, HE WILL
TAKE US OFF THE BENCH.

connected to those around us and that His plan for the world will ultimately be fulfilled as we allow Him to use us according to His timetable.

We are not pawns, but vital players on God's team. When He needs us in the lineup, He will take us off the bench. God planned the lives of Abraham and Moses as well as the 12 original disciples in order to fit into the unfolding of eternity. Similarly, our divine delays are not merely about *our* needs and *our* desires. A popular phrase puts it this way: "It's not about you." God sometimes uses the burdens of our hearts to birth a larger solution to the burden of *His* heart.

Living with the knowledge of what happened in the past can bring us comfort and hope. Living with the reality of today can motivate us to be realistic. But living with the right perspective of tomorrow offers enormous and limitless possibilities. If snapshots from the past are any indication of the blessings that come disguised as divine delays, then it's important that we review a short list of what we can expect.

- Like Abraham and Sarah, we could receive our promise from God, experience laughter in our latter years, and become the recipient of inexplicable blessings.

- Like Joseph, who endured a tremendous season of delay, we may eventually be elevated to a position of influence and have an impact on an entire nation with the wisdom we've earned through our time spent in the waiting room.

- Like Zechariah and Elizabeth, who became the parents of John the Baptist when they were well along in age, God may use us to make a dynamic deposit into the next generation.

• Like Lazarus, who was raised from the dead after three days, a dramatic deliverance based on our delay may help our family and friends rise to a new level of faith in Christ.

DOWN FOR THE COUNT

Most people don't realize that even Jesus experienced a divine delay. He spent three days in the tomb, with the wounds of spiritual and physical warfare all over His body. His head was bruised and scarred beyond recognition. His hands, His feet and His side were pierced through and through. For three long days, He laid on a cold slab of stone. It was dark in that cave. It was lonely. All of His friends and family members had scattered. They were in a state of shock. And I'm sure that even Satan believed that Christ was down for the count. It likely appeared to everyone that Jesus was defeated and that the ultimate dagger and deathblow were firmly in place.

I have often wondered why God allowed His only Son to remain in that condition for three long days. Why didn't the Father simply resurrect His Son immediately after He laid His life down? It would have been so easy for the Almighty to do this. It would have been so effortless. Thankfully, the Savior knew the end from the beginning. Unlike Jesus, we are not blessed with such omniscience. Instead, when in the midst of a divine delay, we find ourselves asking such desperate questions as: *Why me? Why now? Why this? Lord, am I down for the count?*

My husband and I were married before I graduated from college. We exchanged wedding vows on a hot, rainy day in July. I returned to school that fall but also held down a job to help make ends meet. Soon, David received an offer for a better position in another part of New Jersey. So we relocated to Northern New Jersey to be closer to his new engineering job. But the cost of living was much higher than where we had been living in South Jersey.

Because of our financial needs as newlyweds, I was unable to take more classes right away. To my disappointment, the dream of fulfilling my college education was put on hold. Two years later, I became pregnant with our first child, Danielle, and the dream was put on hold again. The years passed, and we had another child, Jessica. By this time, David had transitioned from a career in engineering to full-time Christian ministry, so I took on responsibilities in the church, and the dream was put on hold once again. Before I knew it, two decades were in my rearview mirror, and while I could see that my family life and ministry had flourished, some of the other areas of my life seemed to have died on the vine.

There were other dreams in my heart that also had to be put on hold during this time. One such dream was God's calling on my life to travel itinerantly and participate in missionary journeys to other countries. Since David was often away on such trips, well-meaning people would frequently ask me, "Why don't you travel more?" Looking back, the question made me feel as if I was doing something wrong or was not being spiritual enough. Each time this question was voiced, I would pray for God's wisdom to guide me in my choices. Thankfully, I recognized that our children were my top priority and that when my husband traveled I was able to hold down the fort at home. At that time, I did not feel released by God to leave our children with friends or family. My thought was that opportunities for ministry would always be around, but my girls would not. Deep in my heart, though, I knew that I was in the throes of a divine delay.

Just when I was about to give up on my academic dreams, an unbelievable opportunity to return to school fell into my lap. I applied and was accepted into a graduate program in divinity that made allowance for people such as me who had many years of ministry experience and several years of college, but who had been unable to complete the bachelor's degree. In addition, because of the contribution of my ministry and that of my husband's to the betterment of society within the greater New York region, the school waived my tuition. Alleluia! God's blessings and timing could not have been better.

IS YOUR DELAY DIVINE OR DESERVED?

Just as there are divine delays, there are also *deserved* delays. With deserved delays, our prayers and plans fail to materialize because of (1) a lack of faith, (2) foolish actions, or (3) presumptuous thinking. Let's look more closely at these reasons for deserved delays.

1. Lack of Faith

Faith is clearly one of the most important concepts in the entire New Testament. In God's economy, faith is the required currency that allows us to receive His promises into our lives. This is why the writer of the book of Hebrews exhorts, "And without faith it is impossible to please God, because anyone who comes to him must believe that he exists and that he rewards those who earnestly seek him" (Heb. 11:6, *NIV*). Not only is faith a necessity in pleasing God, it is also a vehicle through which we receive rewards from the Lord. Because faith is God's currency, the lack of faith speaks of a life that is spiritually poor and devoid of bartering power before the Lord.

Lack of faith can certainly be the cause of a deserved delay. I will pick up on this point in a moment, but first I want to make sure that I'm being completely clear about this dimension of faith, which many scholars call "living faith." Living faith is the tool that God gives us to obtain His promises.

The Bible tells us in Mark 9:23 that "anything is possible if a person believes" (*NLT*). In other words, living faith means that we trust that God is both *willing* and *able* to answer our prayers. It means that we abandon all trust in our own resources and abilities and trust God to do what we cannot do for ourselves. This kind of faith is expressed when we lay hold of the promises of God by trusting Him for an outcome based on a biblically sound promise, such as the ones found in Psalm 23: "The Lord is my shepherd; I have everything I need. He lets me rest in green meadows; he leads me beside peaceful streams. He renews my strength. He guides me along right paths, bringing honor to his name" (vv. 1-3, *NLT*). Living faith implies complete reliance upon God and full obedience to His will.

In addition to living faith, there is also "saving faith." Saving faith occurs when we trust in the saving work of Jesus Christ. Saving faith is central to the New Testament. It is the belief that God sent His Son to become the Savior of the world and that Jesus Christ bought humanity's salvation by dying an atoning death on Calvary's cross. It occurs when we abandon all reliance on our own efforts to gain salvation. It is our recognition that salvation cannot be attained by good deeds, ethical decency or by any other means. It is the attitude of completely trusting in Christ and depending on Him alone for salvation. When the Philippian jailer asked, "Sirs, what must I do to be saved?" (Acts 16:30, *NLT*), Paul and Silas unhesitatingly answered, "Believe on the Lord Jesus and you will be saved" (v. 31, *NLT*). Through saving faith, people receive salvation.

In the context of divine delays, therefore, a lack of faith occurs when we are unable to fully believe in God's ability to answer our prayers—in other words, when we have a lack of *living faith*. A lack of this type of faith is a real obstacle to answered prayer. The writer of the book of James puts it this way:

If you need wisdom—if you want to know what God wants you to do—ask him, and he will gladly tell you. He will not resent your asking. But when you ask him, be sure that you really expect him to answer, for a doubtful mind is as unsettled as a wave of the sea that is driven and tossed by the wind. People like that should not expect to receive anything from the Lord. They can't make up their minds. They waver back and forth in everything they do (Jas. 1:5-8, *NLT*).

Despite our level of high commitment to the Lord, we are instructed that our faith must be expressed if we are to see and enjoy God's answers to prayers. It is conclusive: The lack of faith can cause a deserved delay.

2. Foolish Actions

The second reason we may experience a deserved delay is because of our own foolish actions. When we do things that go against biblical wisdom, practical wisdom or sound judgment, the result may be a delay (or even a denial) to our plans and desires.

Heartaches and headaches are always the result of decisions made on the basis of emotion or poor planning. In Matthew 25: 1-13, Jesus tells the story of 10 bridesmaids who took their lamps and went to meet the bridegroom. Five of the bridesmaids were foolish and took no oil for their lamps. When the bridegroom was delayed until midnight, the foolish bridesmaids ran out of oil for their lamps and had to go to a shop to buy some more. In the meantime, the bridegroom arrived and took the five wise brides-maids to the marriage feast. Later, when the five foolish brides-maids arrived, they were denied entrance to the marriage feast.

These five bridesmaids were foolish because they did not plan or prepare for what was ahead. As a result, they missed out on one of those once-in-a-lifetime opportunities. If you want to avoid being like the foolish bridesmaids, there are three things you must do: (1) have a plan; (2) know what steps to take to advance the plan; and (3) don't expect God to do for you what you should do for yourself.

3. Presumptuous Thinking

The third reason why our prayers and plans may deserve to be delayed is because of presumptuous thinking. To "presume" means to take something for granted or make a faulty assumption that God wants us to have or do a particular thing when there is no biblical basis for this belief. People sometimes act on impulses or ignorance and do things that God never intended. As a result, they find themselves in sticky or even dangerous situations.

What is at the root of presumption? It stems from a lack of knowledge of God's Word and His ways. Presumption always leads to a life dominated by speculation and assumption. In 2 Samuel 6:1-7, the Ark of the Lord was being transported to Jerusalem on a new cart. (The Ark of the Lord was a wooden box overlaid with gold; it contained several items that were sacred and highly revered by the Jewish people.) This was a joy-filled day in the region, and there was a celebration engulfing the event. As the people were celebrating and rejoicing, the oxen pulling the cart stumbled. Uzzah, a man who was helping move the Ark, reached out to keep the Ark from falling. When he touched the box, he was instantly struck dead by the Lord.

Uzzah presumed that it was his responsibility to keep the Ark from falling to the ground. Although his desire to keep the Ark from damage or disgrace was honorable, Jewish law clearly stated that only the priests were permitted to touch the ark. Uzzah was mistaken about the scope of his responsibilities. He was not a priest, and his presumption led not only to his death but also to the delay of the Ark coming to Jerusalem. Like Uzzah, people who live presumptuously rarely discover God's best for

their lives. Solid knowledge of God's ways comes only by regularly reading and studying His Word.

THE FAMOUS FOUR

Well-meaning (albeit ill-informed) people generally offer four
primary causes for delayed answers to prayer. I call these reasons
the "Famous Four." The first cause for delay that they will often
tell you is that "God is waiting for you to pray more." Of course,
praying harder and longer is not always the cure in times of distress. If this were true, sick loved ones would never die, and any
couple who wanted to have a baby would have one.

A second reason for delays that these individuals will tell you
is that "God is trying to give you more patience." What they really mean is that God wants to see just how long you will hold on
before giving up. Patience is only one of the lessons you can
learn from waiting. God is divine, so pat answers to tough questions rarely satisfy a soul longing for wisdom.

The third reason for divine delays that these people often give
is that the delay is intended to test your faith. But, as we have
seen, divine delays are not always connected to lack of faith.

And the fourth and final off-the-cuff reason that people give for
divine delays is that delays are designed as a test of your character.

Each of these reasons would make a great phrase for a
bumper sticker. But remember, divine delays are ordained and
orchestrated by God. They are not necessarily caused by the need
for us to do more or do better. God's timing is the key. God
ordains postponements and uses them to expand our sphere of
influence. Simply put, God withholds things from us in order to
make the best use of us—right where we are. God knows that
moving us forward at the wrong time would disrupt His divine
design for us and for the people around us. We are a part of
God's universal plan for the people in our sphere of influence.

And it is very likely that we are right where God wants us to be.

It is also quite likely that we are already in the right place at the right time. This statement is not meant as an excuse for procrastination but as an important perspective for those who are frustrated and feeling as if they've failed somehow. In the process of divine delays, our perspective determines our posture, and our posture determines our power to live a life of purpose.

Perspective is everything, and recognizing that we are in the right place at the right time certainly has its advantages. For instance, in my own life, because I learned to wait on the Lord, I did not have to compromise my walk with the Lord by settling for Tom. In the same way, God opened a door for me in seminary because I was at the right place at the right time.

GAINING GOD'S PERSPECTIVE

If you are experiencing a divine delay, you need to understand the real reasons for this season in your life. You must see yourself as God's man or God's woman for the hour, and you must understand that God has you right where He needs you to be—even though you may feel frustrated and forgotten. It has been said that when God closes one door in our lives, He opens up another door. Imagine that between the two doors is a long hallway. You need to be aware that it can be hell in the hallway! This is because the door behind you has closed and the door in front of you has yet to open. Only God can open the next door. Your job is to gain God's perspective while you are in the hallway.

Waiting Makes Us Worshipers
Everything God does is designed to refine our relationship with Him and with those around us. Divine delays are no exception.

One of the main reasons God permits seasons like these in our lives is to make us better worshipers.

In order to be a worshiper, we must first have a heart of loving surrender toward God. However, growing in that love relationship with God is a process that involves deferred gratification. As a child, I remember how difficult it was for me to wait for my birthday or a special holiday to arrive. If my parents had promised a certain gift on that special day, the waiting was even more difficult. My expectation was high because I knew that my parents would do what they had promised. When the day finally arrived and I received the promised gift, my love for my mom and dad increased exponentially.

Our relationship with the heavenly Father works the same way. When we have the right perspective, waiting lifts our love and our worship to a whole new level. As we keep our eyes on God's faithfulness, waiting for Him moves us closer to His heart. Trusting in another person's faithfulness is a key ingredient in any successful relationship. Some of the people in my life are extremely faithful to me, and whenever I am around them I feel a sense of closeness, love and appreciation. It is the faithfulness of their friendship that causes me to feel intimacy and trust for them. Likewise, when we focus on God's faithfulness, it causes our heart to appreciate the love relationship we have with Him.

If the saying about absence making the heart grow fonder is true, then divine delays should cause our spiritual heart to grow toward God. Perhaps waiting for our prayers to be answered is

EVERYTHING GOD DOES IS DESIGNED TO REFINE OUR RELATIONSHIP WITH HIM AND WITH THOSE AROUND US. DIVINE DELAYS ARE NO EXCEPTION.

one of the methods God chooses to catapult our worship to a new height in how we express God's worthiness in our lives.

I believe that our spiritual heart gets its strength from waiting on God. But when we focus on the gift rather than on the giver, we often end up feeling frustrated, and waiting becomes . . . a weight. This kind of weight can crush even the strongest heart. Thus, in the process of divine delays, we must always ask ourselves the question: Is my heart focusing on the gift when I should be focusing on the faithfulness of the giver? Time spent in a divine delay is never wasted, because our love relationship with God is at the center of His divine design for our lives.

Waiting Makes Us Wiser
There have been times when I pressed the pause button on my DVD player in order to take a closer look at the action going on in the movie. Having control over the pause button empowered me to see the situation from a different perspective. In the same way, when God presses the "pause button" on our lives, it makes us wiser because pausing brings us into God's divine perspective of time, life and priorities.

Having a divine perspective consists of seeing our relationships and responsibilities through the lenses of eternity. God wants us to handle life based on His intended purpose, not on our shortsightedness, selfishness or emotional state. When we look at life through His perspective, we see ourselves not as players in a program but as part of His wonderful eternal plan.

Delays Are Not Denials
Your delay may not be a denial of your request, but rather God simply saying, "Not now." I remember when my husband, David, and I wanted to have our first child. We tried to conceive for a long time with no results. Month after month, our doctor encouraged us not to give up. I must admit that trying was the

easy part—waiting was much harder. We prayed, held on to hope, and believed that God would give us a baby. It was another divine delay.

Around this same time, God was busy opening doors for us to plant a new church. He was about to use us to birth a new body of believers in New Jersey. Somehow, in the middle of all the preparations for the church, I managed to get pregnant. Danielle was born two weeks after the launch of the ministry. She was a sign of a whole new and exciting season of fruitfulness in our lives. All at once, we had become spiritual parents for the people in our fledgling congregation and natural parents to Danielle. I believe that this dual blessing was no coincidence. It was a confirmation and a part of God's divine design for our lives. God was right on time!

When Israel was under bondage to the Babylonians, God gave the prophet Habakkuk a vision of their future freedom. However, because God delayed the manifestation of the vision, Habakkuk became discouraged and complained to the Lord. God responded by saying, "But these things I plan won't happen right away. Slowly, steadily, surely, the time approaches when the vision will be fulfilled. If it seems slow, wait patiently, for it will surely take place. It will not be delayed" (Hab. 2:3, NLT). THE MESSAGE renders the last sentence of this verse this way: "It will be right on time." Delays are not denials, but they do call for staying power.

YOUR SEASON WILL COME

Our life in God consists of seasons. King David recognized this truth when he wrote, "Happy is the man who does not walk in the way sinful men tell him to, or stand in the path of sinners, or sit with those who laugh at the truth. But he finds joy in the Law of the Lord and thinks about His Law day and night. This man is like a tree planted by rivers of water, which gives its fruit at the right time [seasons] and its leaf never dries up. Whatever he does will work out well for him" (Ps. 1:1-3, *NLV*). It really is possible for us to be properly plugged in to God and yet find ourselves waiting by the riverbank. Even when we are like the tree that's firmly planted and well-watered, we will only bear fruit in our proper season.

At the right season, the things stored in God's treasury of delayed blessings will be released. Until then, we must realize that divine delays are not an indicator of a stagnant season but of two very special opportunities. The first opportunity is that of *maturation*. In a divine delay, our perspective about our promise can mature. This delay can result in us seeing things from a higher and nobler perspective. The second opportunity we gain from a divine delay is that we can mature in our view of God's heart concerning the people around us. We tend to see people based on how we're feeling about ourselves and our lives. Consequently, when our thinking shifts due to the dealings of God or the waiting process, the very same people who we used to discount as not being a right fit to aspects of our dreams may start to really blossom and shine. Remember, divine delays are not only about us. They can also be the maturing process we need in order to unlock the destinies of others who've been experiencing their own divine delays.

Both of these maturing opportunities contain precious nuggets of God's love and wisdom—which are hidden in the shadows of divine delays. Gaining an eternal perspective and a greater love for people are important prerequisites for moving forward in God's economy.

Jesus clarified God's divine design for our lives when He said, "You must love the Lord your God with all your heart, all your soul, and all your mind. This is the first and greatest commandment. A second is equally important: 'Love your neighbor as yourself'" (Matt. 22:37-39, *NLT*). Our lives are meant to be a divine expression of God's goals, not our own. We are meant to mark time by focusing on our relationship with God and on our responsibilities to each other. In this day and age, most of us are consumed with merely focusing on tomorrow, rather than on eternity. Yet in this season while we are waiting for God to move, we need to focus on the three precious nuggets of God's love and wisdom, which are sure to mature us.

SURVIVAL SECRETS
Remember

The Picture from the Past: Throughout the ages, God has kept His promises to others, although He appeared to be slow-moving to the men and women involved in those divine delays.

The Practice for the Present: You need to abandon your immediate dreams for the sake of the bigger picture—the one with eternal ramifications.

The Promise for the Future: God plans the end from the beginning, and vice versa. Therefore, the future must always be in view as you walk with the Lord. The writer of Hebrews adds, "But these things I plan won't happen right away. Slowly, steadily, surely, the time approaches when the vision will be fulfilled. If it seems slow, wait patiently, for it will surely take place. It will not be delayed" (Hab. 2:3, *NLT*).

These are just three of the precious nuggets that form the soil from which this book has grown. For the last 20 years, I have served as a mentor, as a messenger of the gospel of Jesus Christ, as a mother, and in many other capacities. I have personally walked scores of people through the frustrations, fears, feelings of failure, and ultimate freedom that accompanies divine delays. As you read on, I will share helpful insights and stories with you as you wrestle with the question of "What is God waiting for?" in the hopes that you will move toward a deeper and more mature spiritual life. These stories will also express reality: tragedy and triumph. My prayer is that as you turn these pages, your heart will also turn and embrace God's divine design hidden within your divine delay.

CHAPTER TWO

Caught in a Heavenly Holding Pattern

MAN MUST RISE ABOVE THE EARTH TO THE TOP OF THE ATMOSPHERE AND BEYOND FOR ONLY THUS WILL HE FULLY UNDERSTAND THE WORLD IN WHICH HE LIVES.
SOCRATES

IT'S WONDERFUL TO CLIMB THE LIQUID MOUNTAINS OF THE SKY, BEHIND ME AND BEFORE ME IS GOD AND I HAVE NO FEARS.
HELEN KELLER

Many times, I've been in an airplane at 30,000 feet in the sky and heard the pilot announce, "Ground control has just put us in a holding pattern until further notice. We'll be unable to land on time because of bad weather on the ground." Since passengers are shielded from the reasons behind this decision, frustration often sets in the moment they hear this announcement. Through no fault of their own, their plans are now up in the air (no pun intended).

At times, divine delays are like being caught in a heavenly holding pattern. They can make us feel like unhappy airplane passengers, because there is nothing that we can do to make a difference or that will bring us any closer to our destination. We're stuck, yet desperate for change. We're sick of the same old scene, yet unable to move away from it. We even become sick of ourselves. It's not long before our emotions become tangled in knots because of the amount of time that is seemingly being wasted.

Solomon, the author of the book of Proverbs, makes it clear that this kind of waiting often brings a heavy weight on our hearts: "Hope deferred makes the heart sick, but when the desire comes, it is a tree of life" (Prov. 13:12, *NKJV*). Air sickness and heart sickness—due to deferred desires—have similar effects on our emotions. Both of these conditions can cause us to loathe our surroundings and reject the very things or people God intended to help us. This loathing leads us to seek out ways to escape the pressures that divine delays often bring.

There have been many times in my life when running away from the three Rs—*relationships, reality* and *responsibilities*—seemed to be the best thing to do. Despite the biblical encouragement that states that "the nights of crying your eyes out give way to days of laughter" (Ps. 30:5), in the midnight hour, my heart ached for a respite. I longed for new surroundings. I lived for new opportunities, new connections and new relationships. Even though my desire for these things was not sinful, I knew in my heart that the timing for them was all wrong. Although my heart-sickness continued, I eventually resolved that my longing was truly for the presence of God and that I needed to see a manifestation of His power in the midst of my divine delay.

The "heart" refers to the center of our thoughts, emotions, personality, spiritual life and character. Longing for God actually prepares the soil of the soul to unconditionally accept His divine ways. David wrote, "O Lord, I have longed for your salvation, and your law is my delight. Let me live so I can praise you, and may your laws sustain me" (Ps. 119:174-175, *NLT*). This longing for more of God is designed to heighten our hunger for a life that is totally guided by His ways of doing things. This longing of the heart makes it stronger.

In many ways, the design of the human heart gives us a picture of just how strong the spiritual heart can be. The human heart is a hard-working marvel. It can keep beating even if all other nerves are severed. It beats an average of 75 times a minute; 40 million times a year; or 2.5 billion times in a person who lives for 70 years. During each beat, the average adult heart discharges about 4 ounces of blood. This amounts to 3,000 gallons of blood per day, or 650,000 gallons a year—enough to fill the tanks of 81 car tanks of 8,000 gallons each.

The human heart does enough work in 1 hour to lift a 150-pound man to the top of a 3-story building. It expends enough energy in 12 hours to lift a 65-ton tank 1 foot off the ground. It produces enough power in 70 years to lift the largest battleship completely out of the water.[2] The human heart must be well-conditioned and beat strongly in order to sustain physical life. Yet how much stronger and more well-conditioned must our spiritual heart be in order to sustain spiritual life?

Just as the human heart beats in a rhythm, heavenly holding patterns beat out a rhythm, too. If we're not musically inclined, we may not be able to decipher or recognize the melodious beat. Likewise, if we are not spiritually sensitive or willing to look at things from a biblical perspective, we may not be able to discern that divine delays may simply be the holding pattern of heaven that has its own rhythm. Without knowing this tidbit of information about the Lord's ways, divine delays can simply seem as if we're living in a pattern of repeated disappointment. However, if we choose to accept delays solely as disappointments, we must also recognize that disappointments can serve to strengthen our spiritual heart.

This way of thinking is opposite to how most people view the longings of the heart. However, I firmly believe that this perspective is another secret of wisdom found in the classroom of divine delays. Just as the physical heart is the central organ of biological life, our spiritual heart is the central organ to our spiritual existence.

THE DEALINGS OF GOD

Heavenly holding patterns are intended to help us, not hurt us. For safety reasons, an airplane cannot land until air traffic control has every matter under control. Similarly, God helps us during divine delays by dealing with the people and situations around us in preparation for the outpouring of His blessings.

In the book of Exodus, the Israelites were delayed in escaping the clutches of Egyptian slavery because of Pharaoh's pride and greed. God placed His children in a heavenly holding pattern as He worked to convince Pharaoh to let them go. While God worked on Pharaoh's heart, He also revealed His heart to the Israelites. As we examine this picture from the past, there are four things we must learn to do: (1) recognize the finger of God; (2) stay in the air; (3) continue circling; and (4) don't blame people on the ground.

1. Recognize the Finger of God
The finger of God is a finger of challenge; it is a pointer to truth. Heavenly holding patterns allow time for the finger of God to touch the hearts of the people around us. It was during the plague of gnats that the Egyptian occultists proclaimed, "This is

GOD HELPS US DURING DIVINE DELAYS BY DEALING WITH THE PEOPLE AND SITUATIONS AROUND US IN PREPARATION FOR THE OUTPOURING OF HIS BLESSINGS.

the finger of God" (Exod. 8:19, *NIV*). That is a remarkable statement, especially when we consider its source. These Egyptian occultists recognized that the power of God was the source for the release of a plague of gnats. Pharaoh, however, could not recognize this fact because his heart was hardened. And through the hardness of his heart, he made life for the Israelites a nightmare.

In God's quest to open Pharaoh's eyes to the need to liberate the Israelites, He set numerous plagues upon Egypt. In the same way, God may be using your divine delay to get a message across to others. (I recognize that God does not use wicked, demonic practices to instruct or guide people, but He can still thwart the plans of people so that His overarching goal is accomplished.) God's message during the difficulties that often arise in the lives of the people around us during a divine delay reveals the reality of His sovereignty in the earth.

As God works on the hearts of those around you, stay out of His way. Don't gloat. Don't rejoice when you see others being touched by the finger of God. Remember that it's not all about you, but that it's all about God working out His eternal purposes in the earth and in the hearts of people.

2. Stay in the Air

In aeronautical lingo, a holding pattern is referred to as airborne parking. The aircraft is flown in a racetrack pattern, around and around, until there is space or opportunity in the system for the aircraft to move on to the next segment of the flight. A heavenly holding pattern exists when a particular cycle of life repeats itself over and over again. It is a state of inaction, with no progress and no change. When we are in a heavenly holding pattern, we often feel as though our challenges will never give way to change. But some challenges can only be resolved by God's intervention. And while God is working to bring change around us, we are left to simply "park it in the air."

Airborne parking requires some highly technical skills. In aeronautical terms, before you can fly a "hold," you have to work out how to get into the pattern. In some cases, this may require changing direction in order to get the aircraft flying in the correct direction. The way you join the hold is governed by the direction from which you enter it. Working this out may be more difficult than actually flying the hold itself. In addition, there may be an aircraft 1,000 feet above or below you doing the very same thing. Therefore, it is critical that you stay at your assigned altitude while engaging in a holding pattern.

The only way to join the hold and stay in the air during a heavenly holding pattern is to daily *begin with the end in mind.* Beginning with the end in mind is done by starting each day with the truth that God is using the burden of your heart to address a surprisingly larger burden of His own heart. It is also accomplished by recognizing that your divine delay is positioning you to significantly impact the people in your sphere of influence. Maintaining this perspective is a key in gaining a proper attitude during your divine delay. This mind-set requires that you constantly change the directions of your thoughts. When this happens, you are able to enter the hold in the right direction.

The key to beginning again with the end in mind is to realize that you are already in the sky, recognize that things have gotten off the ground, remember that you are nearing the end of the delay, and repeatedly look around to see the big picture. Having these ideas in mind will ensure that you stay in the air.

3. Keep Circling

Managing repetition is no easy feat. Doing the same things over and over again without getting closer to God or to our purpose can be a discouraging process. In times like these, our reliance on biblical promises, well-laid plans and an eternal perspective may appear to make little or no sense at all. The temptation to resign from life becomes a daily struggle. Living in a holding pattern can sometimes make us wonder if we are being realistic, foolish or fanatical. Divine delays test our spiritual digestive system to see if we can stomach self-doubt. Yet this process is not intended to cause us to *throw up*, but rather to *grow up*.

Our lives are meant to be like fruitful vines, giving life to those around us. But just as a tree needs time to mature before it can give life, so too our hopes need time to mature before they can fit into God's divine design. In other words, our desires need time to become fully grown. That's right: Our desires need time to grow into productive structures that others can pick and eat from.

If a desire is not processed in a healthy way, it can become a dangerous thing. It can become a monster or a monkey on your back. It can drive you to deal with relationships and responsibilities in self-destructive ways. Our desires have the ability to color how we see ourselves and the world around us. An immature desire is like a half-baked idea. It has not taken all the ramifications of its impact on others into consideration. It's not ripe. It's unfit to be used. The only remedy for a half-baked desire is to keep it on the burner until it is fit for human consumption.

How do we deal with the frustration of being on the back burner of life? The key is endurance. Endurance is an aggressive, courageous attitude that is needed during the hard times of divine delays. It is a mind-set that rejects self-pity. Endurance rules out discouragement no matter how hopeless the situation appears to be.

I recently came across the following true story that illustrates the nature of endurance: On December 7, 1914, Ernest Shackleton and a crew of 28 men aboard a ship named Endurance entered the packed ice off the continent of Antarctica. Their goal was to become the first party to trek across the continent on foot. It was a goal they would never achieve. Nearly a century later, the tale of

Endurance remains one of the most fascinating examples of human triumph in the face of adversity.

The Endurance sailed through the ice until January 18, 1915, when the ship was trapped in the crushing ice of the Antarctic pack. Despite the efforts of the crew, the Endurance remained lodged in the ice for the next nine months. The thick ice of the Antarctic pack pressed constantly, threatening to crush the ship to splinters. This threat of failure and death forced the crew to abandon the ship in October 1915. From then on, the party lived on the ice. One month later, the ship sank, stranding the crew with minimal stores and three short-boats on the drifting pack ice. The men survived for the next six months, killing seals, penguins and, ultimately, their own sled dogs for food.

In April 1916, the 28 men spotted an island on the horizon. The ice flow broke just enough to allow them to put to sea in some of the roughest waters on Earth. Seven days later, they landed on the uninhabited and inhospitable Elephant Island. However, Shackleton knew that because they were now far from regular shipping lanes, the chances of a rescue from their location were nonexistent. His crew may have been on land, but they were far from safe—and farther from home. So on April 24, 1916, he set sail with a crew of five men for the populated island of South Georgia, which was 800 miles away.

Shackleton and his crew sailed for 17 days, navigating by sextant and fighting their way through high seas of freezing water. Finally, they made it. They reached South Georgia Island! The weather and their own tattered condition required them to land on the uninhabited side of the island. Shackleton and two other men were then forced to trek on foot across the island. It took 36 hours for them to traverse 22 miles across the glacier-clad, thousand-foot high mountains to reach the whaling port of Stromness. Shackleton and his men finally arrived at the port on May 20, 1916. His attempts to rescue his crewmen left behind on Elephant Island would not be successful until August 30, 1916, a full 22 months after they had initially set out. Remarkably, all 28 men survived the ordeal.[3]

The next time you face a divine delay that seems impossible to cope with, remember the story of the Endurance . . . and press on. The captain and crew demonstrated incredible ability to forge through all kinds of weather, disappointments and emotional setbacks in order to survive and stay connected. Likewise, divine delays are not dealt with by taking the easiest path, but by taking consistent and persistent action until your heart has resolved to accept God's divine timing for your life.

4. Don't Blame the People on the Ground

While in the midst of a divine delay, we must recognize that the delay is not someone else's fault. When life is less than livable, it's natural to accuse those around us for the trouble we're facing. Blame-shifting has become a national pastime.

Instead of holding themselves responsible in tough times, more Americans now blame others. In past economic depressions in America, murder rates went down while suicides went up, because Americans—trained in the puritan ethic of self-reliance and internal restraint—blamed themselves for personal economic failure. Today, when people reach a breaking point in frustration, they are more likely to lash out at others.[4]

Whenever we are in a heavenly holding pattern, the first thing we may want to do is whip out our pointing finger, aim it and fire at someone—anyone. However, as passengers on the airplane being held in the heavenly holding pattern, we are not calling the shots. God is the divine air traffic controller, and He has the authority to determine our future movements. Daniel 2:20-21 states, "For wisdom and might are His. And He changes the times and the seasons" (NKJV). Relief can only come when we recognize that the One who is in charge of our delay is the One who clears the skies for our safe passage—the Lord Almighty.

Blaming the world systems, the past, or the people around us leads only to deception and discord. The people around us are not our problem. Maintaining a godly perspective during a divine delay leads to satisfying relationships with friends and others. Having God's viewpoint of our holding pattern will help us to make good decisions as we deal with the possible relational strains. When we embrace a godly perspective about our season, we will break away from our tendency to put the fault on others and end the blame game.

THE KEYS TO SMOOTH SAILING

There are two keys that we need to keep in mind when we attempt to change the direction of our relationships from turbulence to smooth sailing during a divine delay: (1) relationships require hindsight; and (2) relationships require commitment.

Key #1: Relationships Require Hindsight

Many, many years ago in Park Rapids, Minnesota, a homeless person walked into a restaurant and asked the owner for a free meal. The traveler looked so hungry and disheveled that the sympathetic restaurant owner said, "Okay, what'll ya have?" The man sat down at a table and had a good meal—a first-class handout.

As the traveler was leaving, he walked up to the owner and even bummed a cigarette. As the traveler fished in a pocket for a

WHEN WE EMBRACE A GODLY PERSPECTIVE ABOUT OUR SEASON, WE WILL BREAK AWAY FROM OUR TENDENCY TO PUT THE FAULT ON OTHERS AND END THE BLAME GAME.

match, he carelessly pulled out a 20-dollar bill.

"Say, what's that," shouted the proprietor. "You come in here bumming a meal, and you've got 20 bucks?" The owner grabbed the twenty.

"But this was supposed to be a free meal," the traveler protested.

"Not on your life," said the restaurant man. "I'll just take 35 cents out of this twenty."

The traveler said, "Just remember, buddy, I don't want you to do this. I'm not asking you."

"Izzat so?" the owner shot back as he handed the traveler 19 dollars and 65 cents in change.

The unhappy ending of the story is that when the owner took the money to the bank, he discovered that the 20-dollar bill he had taken from the homeless man was counterfeit.[5]

Hindsight is the wisdom gained from an event after it has already taken place. The owner's perspective of the homeless man changed once he realized that the man really was penniless because all he had was a counterfeit twenty. Even though the owner was angry about the counterfeit bill, he could not call the traveler a liar, because the man had repeatedly tried to warn him. Sometimes, during a divine delay, we must use hindsight to change our perspective of the people in our past.

Key #2: Relationships Require Commitment

Cleaning out the refrigerator is one of the most unpleasant of household chores. There have been times when I've found left-over food growing green fuzzy mold. The only thing you can do with this rotten leftover food is to throw it away.

Unlike spoiled food, relationships should not be thrown away during a divine delay. We need to learn to separate out the value of the person versus the relational pain that may have arisen from offenses or awkward circumstances surrounding our bout with divine delay. As in the case of spoiled food, the food may have tasted great when it was first prepared, just like new relationships may have initially been satisfying. But when relationships are ignored due to the distractions divine delays can create, they suffer and result in pain. Addressing the pain must become the focus of our commitment and not the lesser route of abandoning the relationship, which may be more tempting.

In order to adequately address the pain and renew our commitment to the relationship, vital soul work is needed. If we ignore the pain, our past offenses can become mixed up with our present fears and frustrations, resulting in what I call "resentment rollover." This is resentment that has nothing to do with our divine delay but is left over from past disagreements, offenses and unmet needs.

These offenses seem to crop up during bouts with divine delays because we are more prone during these times to critique and exaggerate every area of our life. Since a major aspect of our dream is being delayed and we have no control over it, the parts that can be addressed are often exaggerated. If we are not careful, we may find ourselves over-examining our relationships and finding faults in them simply because the people are in our reach. If we find ourselves doing this, we need to take a step back and realize that the real issue is the divine delay and not necessarily the relationship. If we're not careful of this trap, we may find ourselves becoming resentful of the strained relationship to the point where we begin to consider abandoning our commitment to it.

We were created to enjoy committed relationships, first with God and then with other people. Commitment and community are inseparable. The children of Israel needed to make a fresh commitment to each other and to the Lord while they were in their holding pattern. We must do the same. By simply making a decision to stay dedicated and faithful to our relationships despite our own emotional and mental anguish, we will find the blessings of living in covenant community. These blessings include moral support, empathy and prayer.

COMMITMENT MUST BE FED IN ORDER FOR IT TO FLOURISH

There are also times when commitment must be force-fed. There are two things that we can do to accomplish this: (1) stop shutting up; and (2) stop shutting down emotionally.

Stop Shutting Up

First, we need to stop shutting up, because communication is vital to commitment. Without it, there is no way for hearts to become connected. When it comes to flying an airplane, precise communication becomes vitally important in a holding pattern. To reduce the risk of misunderstanding between the tower and the cockpit, a controller is forbidden to tell a pilot to "hold for takeoff." The mere mention of "takeoff" could trigger a response in the mind of the pilot and cause him to throw the throttles open prematurely.

The correct command is, "Taxi into position and hold." Telling others that we are in a divine delay and that we're taxiing into position so that we can hold on to God's promises for our future is empowering. We should never totally shut up when we are in a holding pattern, as this could cause others to misinterpret our lack of action. Rather, we should tell them that we are not late; we're just waiting for a word from the control tower.

Stop Shutting Down Emotionally

We must also not shut down emotionally. In a divine delay, we tend to disconnect and sink into a state of emotional numbness. This is very common. However, when we shut out others, we also eliminate the balance that fellowship brings to our life.

Living in our own world makes for a life filled with empti-ness. The writer of the book of Ecclesiastes says, "Two are better than one, because they have a good return for their work: If one falls down, his friend can help him up. But pity the man who falls and has no one to help him up!" (Eccles. 4:9-10, *NIV*). This profound passage of Scripture speaks of the power of two. This synergistic power is only released in the context of commit-ment. When we share our life with others, we are able to gain the benefits of collective wisdom and the insight generated within the group.

ENJOY THE RIDE

Whenever I travel on an airplane, I like to watch how older people respond to turbulence or rough landings. If they're accustomed to traveling, they're usually calm and not the least bit afraid. In fact, some even look as though they're enjoying it. They lean back and wait for the plane to land and are not concerned about the danger. Over time, they've learned that in all likelihood, the plane will land safely. Looking at them somehow makes me relax. Heavenly hold-ing patterns provide an opportunity to explore the wonder of God's ability to make us fly high in life.

SURVIVAL SECRETS
Remember

The Picture from the Past: Heavenly holding patterns allow time for the finger of God to touch the hearts of those around you.

The Practice for the Present: While you are going around in circles, God is allowing earthly situations to be prepared for your arrival.

The Promise for the Future: "For wisdom and power are his. He changes times and seasons" (Dan. 2:20-21, *NRSV*).

Notes

1. *The New Bible Dictionary* (Wheaton, IL: Tyndale House Publishers, 1962).
2. Paul Lee Tan, *Encyclopedia of 7,700 Illustrations* (Garland, TX: Bible Communications, Inc., 1996).
3. Jim Allen, Endurance, "Story of Survival, Story of Success." http:/www.Aussieresumes.com.au/newsletter/Archive/August2004.html.
4. Tan, *Encyclopedia of 7,700 Illustrations*.
5. Ibid.

CHAPTER THREE

Frantic About the Future

DELAYS SHINE A DIM LIGHT ON TODAY AND A BLINDING FOG ON OUR HOPES FOR TOMORROW, BUT GOD SEES THROUGH THE DARKNESS AND GUIDES US SAFELY HOME.

Had it not been for the hot July sun scorching my neck, I probably wouldn't have even noticed the weather. While the heat was burning everything in its path, my thoughts were consumed with the looming date of our upcoming second annual women's conference. It was only weeks away, and registrations for the conference had only trickled in. It looked as if just a handful of women would attend. If things did not turn around, we would be tens of thousands of dollars in the red.

I kept wondering how this could have happened. I had invested months of careful planning and prayer into organizing the conference. I had chosen a beautiful venue for the event. The brochures were stylish and informative. And the speakers were well-known, dynamic communicators. In addition, last year's conference had been an overwhelming success. But I was quickly realizing that I wouldn't be able to rely on any of these things to guarantee the success of this year's conference.

I was frantic. To tell you the truth, I really wanted to forget the whole thing and just drop out of serving as the conference host. But I remembered that God had impressed upon me three years earlier that the women in our region and in our church needed to come together for encouragement and teaching. I also remembered that it was God who had given me the vision for the conference. I decided then that the only way to move ahead was by trusting Him to bless it. From that day forward, I reminded God daily that this was *His* idea. I told Him that it was *His* problem. Then I told Him that *He* needed to take care of it. (After such an ugly tantrum, it's a wonder that I'm still alive.)

The days passed and nothing changed. A sinking feeling began to take root in the pit of my stomach. The fear of failure and embarrassment loomed over my head like a dark cloud. I consoled myself by saying that I was only doing what I was told. This trick did not fool my feelings, however. I just couldn't seem to get my emotions to buy the story my mind was trying to sell to them.

Around this time, I spent a week at Rick Warren's church in sunny California to attend the Purpose Driven Worship Conference and Festival. I was there to receive an award for a worship song that I had entered in the church's international Song Seeker contest. But because of the issues surrounding the conference, my stress level was going through the roof.

My friend Pamela and I were sharing a hotel room during the festival. The music and choral directors from my church were also along for the trip. Yet though I was surrounded by friends, I kept my stressful heart a secret. Each morning at around 4:00 A.M., I'd awake feeling overwhelmed by the pressure to make the conference a success. I'd quietly slip out of bed, grab my Bible and carefully tiptoe into the bathroom to pray.

Have you ever tried praying when your mind and heart was tied in knots? In the stillness of the dawn, I found myself complaining to God rather than praying to Him. "Why is it taking so long for registrations to come in?" I would say. "What am I doing wrong? When will my prayers be answered?" Right there, in the midst of my tearful murmurings, my heavenly Father confirmed in my heart His ability to see me through this challenge. But He let me know He would do it His way—not mine.

That's not quite what I wanted to hear. You see, I wanted an overnight miracle. I wanted hundreds of women to immediately call in their registrations. Instead, what I received was a reminder from the Holy Spirit of this passage of Scripture: "God is not a man, that he should lie, nor a son of man, that he should change his mind. Does he speak and then not act? Does he promise and not fulfill?" (Num. 23:19, *NIV*).

With tears flowing from my bloodshot eyes, I quickly remembered what I had forgotten—that when God makes a decision, He does not vacillate on it; when God speaks, He does not lie; and whatever God promises, He will perform. I remembered that I could trust Him.

I want to remind you of that fact, too. When God places you in a divine delay, there's no need to become frantic about the future. In the end, the conference was a great success in spiritual vitality and attendance. The lives of the women were radically changed for Christ. Shaky marriages were stabilized and hurting hearts were healed. To top it off, our income exceeded the cost of the conference. That long, hot summer, I learned that if I simply do what God tells me to do, He will take care of the rest.

Doing what God tells us to do is not always easy. Ignoring God's instructions is especially tempting when we are being taken advantage of at work, when we're hurting, when we're broke, or when we feel that our marriage or children are sucking all of the life out of us. Waiting is also hard when our emotions are running high and it seems logical to do what's most convenient. But in the midst of a delay, we need to take the high road and do what God tells us to do. This road is easiest when we know the secrets of avoiding frantic feelings. The Bible supplies such secrets.

Besides being Israel's first ruler, King Saul was also a skillful warrior. Following a victory over some 30,000 Philistine troops, Saul was instructed to wait for the prophet Samuel in a place called Gilgal. Rather than waiting, Saul became impatient and went ahead with his own plans. He was so frantic about the future that his impatience ultimately caused him to lose his crown. Saul's future would have been secured had he been aware of three important principles: (1) Always keep appointments with God; (2) don't try to force the future; and (3) commit to the daily practice of fearless living.

ALWAYS KEEP APPOINTMENTS WITH GOD

Keeping our appointment with God means that we must continue to wait even when He seems late. If you're like me, you don't like being stood up for a meeting. It's especially painful when the encounter we are expecting is with a beloved friend.

Continue to Wait Even When God Seems Late
It is important to understand how critical it is to keep our appointments with God during a season of waiting. Our destiny depends on it. Read carefully Samuel's words when he arrives at Gilgal and realizes that Saul did not wait long enough:

> "That was a fool thing to do," Samuel said to Saul. "If you had kept the appointment that your God commanded, by now God would have set a firm and lasting foundation under your kingly rule over Israel. As it is, your kingly rule is already falling to pieces. God is out looking for your replacement right now. This time he'll

do the choosing. When he finds him, he'll appoint him leader of his people. And all because you didn't keep your appointment with God" (1 Sam. 13:13-14).

In this rebuke, God wanted Saul to understand that when we wait on the Lord, we can be assured of our reward. Conversely, if we don't keep our date with God, He may just find someone else to take our place in His plan.

Have you ever heard the saying, "An opportunity of a lifetime must be seized during the lifetime of the opportunity"? This means that we must take advantage of a great deal or an amazing chance before it is too late. But during divine delays, opportunities of a lifetime coincide with God's timeline. If we grow impatient and move out of God's timing, then we, like Saul, may miss out on God's plan for our life. Saul thought that he was going to lose out on tomorrow—when all the while God wanted to help him gain a slice of forever.

Saul didn't wait long enough. Instead, he took the low road and did what was convenient. Maybe there have been times when you've exchanged obedience for convenience. Most of us have attempted what I call "drive-by obedience." This happens when we make a quick decision based on its ease or what's at hand rather than on God's commands. Drive-by obedience is borne out of fear of losing out on a rare opportunity. In the heat of the moment, we think, *This is my big break! I'd better act now because I may never have this chance again.* But later, when we look back on the decision, we recognize that it wasn't a big break but merely disobedience to God.

Rather than opting for disobedience, we need to take a step back in the moment of decision and harness those feelings of wild impatience. We need to think about what we'd lose by giving in to the temptation. Our ultimate destiny could be at stake, and we may not be able to "unring" the bell.

If the opportunity being presented is truly a God opportunity and not just a good opportunity, then it will surely and eventually show its true colors. So, there's no need for us to settle for drive-by obedience. God is behind the scenes, working out our tomorrows—today. He is arranging things in our life that will have lasting impact. Remember God's generous and loving character and gain encouragement from it, because "just to remember God is a blessing—now and tomorrow and always" (Ps. 113:2).

Overlook Your Options

Another secret to keeping our appointments with God is to *overlook* our options. That's right! We can't allow ourselves to be distracted by creative solutions that can lead to disobedience. While we are waiting for God, we can become inundated with new ideas that appear to fit as the perfect solution to our problems. Yet we need to be aware that these alternatives may not be part of God's plan for our lives.

Also, our impatience could very well cause us to end up like Abraham and Sarah—with an Ishmael on our hands. Ishmael was the son that Abraham had with another woman because he and his wife grew impatient in awaiting for God's promise for a son. Keeping our appointments with God keeps us on track to reaching the dawning of our dream. It's like making an investment. We need to make a serious effort to overlook the quick-fix options, because they won't be profitable in the long-term.

IF THE OPPORTUNITY BEING PRESENTED IS TRULY A GOD OPPORTUNITY AND NOT JUST A GOOD OPPORTUNITY, THEN IT WILL SURELY AND EVENTUALLY SHOW ITS TRUE COLORS.

Waiting makes us a bigger person on the inside. In Romans 8:24-25, Paul says, "That is why waiting does not diminish us, any more than waiting diminishes a pregnant mother. We are enlarged in waiting. [But] we, of course, don't see what is enlarging us. But the longer we wait the larger we become, and the more joyful our expectancy." If we keep on waiting, our faith will become larger than any obstacle in front of us.

DON'T TRY TO FORCE THE FUTURE

Everybody loves a success story. If you look at King Saul's rise to power, you'll see that it was meteoric. He quickly went from a life of obscurity to life in the limelight in Israel. Yet Saul's life in the fast lane failed to prepare him for the pressures associated with greatness.

Quick success can sometimes reveal our hidden insecurities, including jealousy, envy, low self-esteem and greed. Someone once said, "Success will cause the real you to be seen." On the other hand, when we rise slowly to our appointed place of power, we can learn to manage our fears and insecurities along the way. Applying patience to our problem enables the enlarging work of the Spirit of God to take root in our life. James 1:4 encourages us with these words: "So don't try to get out of anything prematurely. Let [patience] do its work so you become mature and well-developed, not deficient in any way." Saul's Achilles' heel was reflected in his need to force his way into the future. Here, and at other times, he pushed past the restraining influence of the Holy Spirit.

Isn't Saul just like most of us? We, too, want quick success. But sometimes God wants to give it to us slowly. The prophet Zechariah put it this way: "You can't force these things. They only come about through my Spirit" (Zech. 4:6-7). Some successes in life, marriage and finances only come because of the deep and unseen workings of the Holy Spirit. We often need to give the Holy Spirit time to influence our hearts. I have learned that whenever we try to force God's hand, we will always force our way into failure.

Let the Deal Die

A few years ago, David and I wanted to build a new home. We needed more space, and our existing home was simply too small. In addition, David needed a large room for his growing library. We searched for a number of months and finally found a plot of land that, while not perfect, was something we could work with. Time passed, and the construction was progressing when I began to have second thoughts about the timing of the move and with some of the challenges with the land we'd purchased. The Holy Spirit was causing a shift in my desires, and soon I had completely changed my mind about moving.

My biggest concern had to do with our youngest daughter. She was still in high school, and our move would result in a very long daily commute for her on a major highway. I talked it over with David and he agreed with my concerns, but reminded me that we could not get out of the contract without losing a lot of money. So I prayed what I call the "Lord, please get us out of this mess!" prayer.

A short time later, we discovered that the builder had made a number of significant construction and design errors on the house. David and I expressed our disappointment over the bungling of our dream home to the builder. He told us that he wouldn't correct the mistakes, but (much to our surprise) offered to let us out of the deal and to return our down payment. When I heard this, I almost broke out into a dance right there in his office.

Still, since we were accustomed to working out difficult situations, we wrestled with the idea of giving up on a project. We tried to force ourselves to go through with it. But ultimately, we accepted the builder's offer and allowed the deal to die.

It's important that we understand that God does not want us to force our way into things. What He already has planned for us will be still there when we arrive at our destination. Delays often shine a dim light on today and a blinding fog on our hopes for tomorrow, but God sees through the darkness and guides us safely home. In Psalm 37, we read, "Quiet down before GOD, be prayerful before him. Don't bother with those who climb the ladder, who elbow their way to the top. Wait patiently for GOD, don't leave the path. He'll give you your place in the sun" (Ps. 37:7,34).

At first glance, this course of action seems ridiculous. The popular route to promotion and advancement in life is to work feverishly to get all you can, can all you get, and then sit on the can. However, in this passage of Scripture, the term "wait" does not imply idleness. Instead, waiting carries the connotation of engaging in continuous service. Think about it in these terms: When we go to a restaurant for a bite to eat, the person who takes our order is called a *waiter* or a *waitress*. Does that person just stand idly around, waiting inactively? No, they continuously serve us by doing the things we ask. It's the same way when we "wait" on the Lord. Our job is to actively engage ourselves in the moment-by-moment pursuit of pleasing Him by doing what He asks us to do. We just may find, as we wait, that God has a better plan in store for us.

Let God Design Your Future

Some time ago, I heard the story of *The Tale of the Three Trees*. In this fable, the lofty aspirations of an olive tree, an oak tree and a pine tree were brought to life. Each of these trees dreamed of becoming something special. The olive tree dreamed of becoming a finely crafted treasure chest. It wanted to hold gold, silver and precious jewels.

One day, woodsmen chose this particular olive tree and cut it down. The olive tree was thrilled. But as the craftsmen began working, the tree realized that they were not making him into a beautiful treasure chest. Instead, they were making him into a manger to hold food for dirty, smelly animals. The tree was heartbroken. His dreams were shattered. After all those years of waiting in the forest, he ended up feeling worthless and demeaned. But God had a better plan.

In the same way, the oak tree dreamed of becoming a part of a huge ship that would carry important kings across the ocean. When the woodsmen cut down the oak, he was so excited. But as time went on, he realized that the craftsmen were not making him into a huge ship. They were making him into a tiny fishing boat. The oak tree was discouraged and disappointed because he did not know that God had a better plan.

The pine tree lived on top of a high mountain. His only dream was to stand tall and remind people of God's great creation. But in a split second, a bolt of lightning sent the tree tumbling to the ground, destroying its dreams. The woodsmen came and picked the tree up, and then carried it off to the scrap pile. Each of the three trees were frantic about their seemingly washed-up destinies. Not one of their dreams had come to fruition, simply because God had a better plan for their future.

Many years later, Mary and Joseph couldn't find any place to lay their little baby boy. Finally, they found a stable. When Jesus was born, they placed him in a manger made from—you guessed

IF YOU CHOOSE TO WAIT, YOU'LL LEARN THAT DIVINE DELAYS COME WITH THE PROMISE OF A GOOD LIFE—A BETTER LIFE THAN YOU COULD HAVE EVER PLANNED FOR YOURSELF.

it—the olive tree. The olive tree had wanted to hold precious jewels. Now it held the greatest treasure of all time, the Son of God.

A few more years went by and Jesus grew up. One day, he needed a boat to cross to the other side of the lake. He didn't choose a large fancy ship, but a small simple fishing boat made from—you guessed it—the oak tree. The same oak tree that wanted to carry important kings across the ocean now carried the King of kings.

The third tree spent many years in a lumberyard until one Friday morning, Roman soldiers were rummaging through a pile of scrap wood where the discarded pine tree lay. That pine tree just knew that they were going to cut him up for firewood. Much to his surprise, the soldiers cut two pieces out of him and made them into a cross. And it was on this pine tree that Jesus was crucified. That tree is still pointing people to God's love and compassion to this day.[1]

I'm sure, if given the chance, each tree would have designed its future differently. But they could not know the plan of God, and neither can we. The moral of this tale is that all three trees thought that it was too late for them to ever be used in a significant way. However, at the right moment in time, they became vital parts of the greatest story ever told.

You may not understand why you are being held back from your future. You may feel ready to force your way forward. But if you do, you'll likely experience heartache, failure and regret. Conversely, if you choose to wait, you'll learn that divine delays come with the promise of a good life—a better life than you could have ever planned for yourself. I've learned that choosing God's way of doing things always yields God's results. C. S. Lewis reached the same conclusion when he stated, "Now is our chance to choose the right side. God is holding back to give us that chance *to choose*. It won't last forever. We must take it or leave it."[2]

COMMIT TO THE DAILY PRACTICE
OF FEARLESS LIVING

Recently, I learned about a man named Mike Utley, who is a former NFL player. As a starting lineman for the Detroit Lions, his future was bright. He was living a fairytale life, one that he had dreamed about since childhood. Tragically, everything changed one autumn afternoon.

Mike went for a routine block during the fourth quarter of a game held on November 17, 1991, between the Detroit Lions and the Saint Louis Rams. His foot slipped when a defensive linebacker from the Rams grabbed his shoulder pad and pulled him to the ground. As Mike fell, he landed on his head, injuring his sixth and seventh vertebrae. He lay on the turf in excruciating pain. It was later confirmed that Mike was paralyzed. Amazingly, he gave everyone the "thumbs up" sign as he was being carried off the field.

This simple gesture symbolized Mike's hope for recovery. The thumbs-up sign would eventually become the recognized symbol of the *Mike Utley Foundation* and his commitment to making the future more hopeful for others with spinal-cord injuries. Mike obviously believes that there is an upside to tragedy. Each day, he practices patience. On February 15, 1999, after nearly eight years of grueling rehabilitation and tireless work with his foundation, Mike stood up at a hotel in Phoenix, Arizona, and took his first steps since that fateful day in Detroit. His accomplishment serves as inspiration for anyone in a wheelchair wondering about the possibility of walking again. His battle is a delay, not a defeat.[3]

I believe that Mike discovered the secret to becoming fearless about the future. He learned that there is always a greater good buried beneath the surface of our struggles. Former U. S. president Theodore Roosevelt once said, "We fight in honorable

fashion for the good of mankind; fearless of the future; unheed-
ing of our individual fates; with unflinching hearts and
undimmed eyes . . . we battle for the Lord."[4]

Remember the story about the women's conference at the
beginning of this chapter? I trusted in my fears instead of exer-
cising my faith. Fear had set in and, well, you know the rest. If I
had continued to yield to my emotional upheaval, I would have
never known the thrill of seeing others healed and set free. The
battle was not for my benefit as much as it was for the good of
others. Oh, how the option of canceling the women's conference
had looked so inviting to me. Oh, how I was tempted to save face
by pulling the plug on the event. But saving face and walking by
faith seldom go hand in hand.

I love the attitude of Habakkuk, the Old Testament prophet
who decided to look beyond his own emptiness and peer into
God's eternal greatness. He said, "Though the fig tree does not
bud and there are no grapes on the vines, though the olive crop
fails and the fields produce no food, though there are no sheep
in the pen and no cattle in the stalls, yet I will rejoice in the Lord,
I will be joyful in God my Savior" (Hab. 3:17-18, *NIV*). The
prophet's words should inspire each one of us timid and tired
time-travelers to continue trusting in the Lord.

The last time I looked in my backyard, there were no fig
trees or sheep, only some brown grass and amorous squirrels in
search of their next love connection. And my bank account has
at times been as bare as Habakkuk's grape vines and cattle
stalls. In this life, our good times will change into tough times,
but God's worth never changes. In this life, emptiness will
sometimes replace fullness, but we can still be filled with joy
because we have God.

The message of this passage in Habakkuk is that we can maintain an undefeatable resolve by avoiding the temptation to focus
on the fearful things in life. Yes, we must be aware of our pain, but

we shouldn't allow it to keep us from contentment in life.

A remarkable woman by the name of Fanny J. Crosby knew how to walk in fearless anticipation of the future. Her story is a testimony of how contentment makes one fearless. In the book *This Is My Story, This Is My Song,* author S. Trevena Jackson shares Fanny's own words regarding the event that changed her life:

> When about six weeks old I was taken sick and my eyes grew very weak and those who had charge of me poulticed my eyes. Their lack of knowledge and skill destroyed my sight forever. As I grew older they told me that I should never see the faces of my friends, the flowers of the field, the blue of the skies or the golden beauty of the stars. . . . Soon I learned what other children possessed, but I made up my mind to store away a little jewel in my heart which I called "Content."[5]

Although she was blind, Fanny wrote 8,000 hymns, and her music has inspired millions. I wonder if her gift of song would have been as powerful if she were not blind. Perhaps her physical handicap gave her the ability to see into the spiritual realm clearer than people with 20/20 vision. Fanny is flesh-and-blood proof that fear is no match against an undefeatable focus.

From a time long ago, this woman teaches us that contentment comes when we realize the only thing in this world worth our undying gaze is a closer relationship with God. When Fanny was asked if she wished she had not become blind, she replied, "Well, the good thing about being blind is that the very first face I'll see will be the face of Jesus."[6] What an awesome foundation for living fearless of the future.

God wants us to live fearlessly. But fearless living does not happen overnight. We must decide each day to work at it and pursue it. We can't allow any other disposition to make its home in our heart. Jesus put it this way: "Peace I leave with you; My [own] peace I now give and bequeath to you [Stop allowing yourselves to be agitated and disturbed; and do not permit yourselves to be fearful and intimidated and cowardly and unsettled]" (John 14:27, *AMP*). This verse shows us the two parts of fearless living: (1) have the peace of God, and (2) have great persistence against timidity.

We need to begin to daily depend on the kind of peace Jesus maintained as He trusted God to calm and quiet Him during times of agitation. This kind of calm trust grows incrementally as we spend time with God. And this level of trust grows out of the quiet rest we develop from sharing moments with the Father.

We can avoid aborting our destiny by pursuing quietness in God and resting in Him. The word "peace" actually means to come to a place in which we are one again with God. This is the place where desire meets self-discipline; where obedience wins out over convenience; where peace reigns as king. This is the place where our emotions give way to an enlarged perspective— one that rests in the reality that there is more to our life than we can see at this moment in time.

God knows that it's easy to feel intimidated when our coworkers, family and friends are moving forward in their goals and successes while we seem to be standing still. But we can't shrink back. Instead, we need to maintain a dogged fearlessness about the future. Theodore Roosevelt once said:

It is not the critic who counts; not the one who points out how the strong man stumbles, or where the doer of deeds could have done them better. The credit belongs to the one who is actually in the arena, whose face is marred by dust and sweat and blood, who strives valiantly; who errs and comes short again and again; because there is not effort without error and shortcomings; but who does actually strive to do the deed; who knows the great enthusiasm, the great devotion, who spends himself in a worthy cause, who at the best knows in the end the triumph of high achievement . . . so that his place shall never be with those cold and timid souls who know neither victory nor defeat.[7]

It's words like these that help me to live fearlessly before God.

SURVIVAL SECRETS
Remember

The Picture from the Past: You need to keep your appointments with God, because opportunities of a lifetime coincide with God's timeline.

The Practice for the Present: Fearless living does not happen overnight. You must make a concerted effort to become fearless and to persist in that fearlessness.

The Promise for the Future: Your day is coming! "Quiet down before God, be prayerful before him. Don't bother with those who climb the ladder, who elbow their way to the top. Wait Patiently for God, don't leave the path. He'll give you your place in the sun" (Psalm 37:7,34).

Notes
1. Joel Osteen, *Your Best Life Now* (New York: Warner-Faith, 2004).
2. C. S. Lewis, *Mere Christianity* (San Francisco: HarperSanFrancisco, 2001).
3. Luke Sacks, "Mike Utley—Still Giving Thumbs Up," NFLPlayers.com, January 25, 2006. http://www.nflplayers.com/news/news_release.aspx?id=4397.
4. Theodore Roosevelt, "The Case Against the Reactionaries," speech delivered in Chicago, Illinois, on June 17, 1912. http://www.theodore-roosevelt.com/trreactionaries.html.

5. Fanny Crosby, quoted in S. Trevena Jackson, *This Is My Story, This Is My Song* (Greenville, SC: Emerald House Group, 1997).

6. Matt Redman, *The Unquenchable Worshipper* (Ventura, CA: Regal Books, 2001), p. 21.

7. Theodore Roosevelt, "Citizenship in a Republic," speech delivered at the Sorbonne, Paris, on April 23, 1910. http://www.Theodoreroosevelt.org/life/quotes.htm.

CHAPTER FOUR

The Long Shot with a Slingshot

GET READY TO FIGHT, YOU AND THE WHOLE COMPANY THAT'S BEEN CALLED OUT. TAKE CHARGE AND WAIT FOR ORDERS.
EZEKIEL 38:7

SINCE BEFORE TIME BEGAN NO ONE HAS EVER IMAGINED, NO EAR HEARD, NO EYE SEEN, A GOD LIKE YOU WHO WORKS FOR THOSE WHO WAIT FOR HIM.
ISAIAH 64:4

When I was about five years old, I had a frightening and unforgettable encounter with an oversized German shepherd named Kyzer. The very sound of his name made me and my three older brothers quiver in fear. We thought of him as "the animal." Kyzer was so fierce that our neighbors kept him barricaded in a large doghouse made of concrete and iron. His bark boomed like a bullhorn.

One day while we were playing in our backyard, "the animal" appeared out of nowhere. There he was, only a few feet away, crouching, growling and snarling—ready to devour us like a four-course meal. When we realized the danger we were in, my wonderfully protective older brothers took off running like bolts of lightning. Unfortunately, there was no way for my chubby little legs to escape the inevitable. Kyzer caught up with me, ignored my screams for mercy, and knocked me down to the ground. I remember seeing my life flash before my eyes (all five years of it).

There I lay, terrified and waiting for Kyzer to take a huge chunk out of me. Instead, he only licked my legs. That was the day that my fear of Kyzer, "the animal," died, because I realized that his bark in no way compared to his bite.

Most of us face what I call "giant faith killers" in the early stages of a divine delay. These are obstacles that appear to dwarf our ability to trust in the power of God. Giant faith killers hinder our ability to see beyond our present circumstances, thus creating a shortsighted view of the future. This type of myopia is typical of people waiting for God. But, as in my experience with Kyzer, giant faith killers rarely live up to their reputations.

In the Bible, David was a young, inexperienced and not-so-soon-to-be king. No one expected him to become a giant-slayer or the ruler of a nation. He was simply a shepherd boy with a slingshot and some rocks. Yet early in his journey, he intentionally took a risk and went after the giant Goliath. It was a daring decision. It was a choice that could have ended in disaster. But David's actions reflect how a person can become a long shot in God's slingshot.

A long shot is a contender who is unlikely to win in a contest. A long shot is also a venture that involves great risk but promises great rewards. Divine delays can make us the most unlikely candidates for a life filled with meaning and significance. Most of us who fall into this category believe that our future is at risk and that the likelihood of us having success is pretty much a long shot. From our viewpoint, a meaningful life is not possible because of our limited abilities, limited finances or limited opportunities. These boundaries hover over our faith and prevent us from seeing and hearing God. But we should not doubt God's ability to do the impossible. Proverbs 3:34 states,

"He gives proud skeptics a cold shoulder, but if you're down on your luck, he's right there to help."

God wants to propel us forward through a divine display of His goodness in our life. Like the rock from David's slingshot, He will shoot us into the lives of people who need our skills, experiences and unique touch. He does this despite the perception that we are Mr. or Ms. Most Unlikely to Succeed.

SEEING THROUGH THE EYES OF GOD

Happy is the man or woman who sees his or her life from God's vantage point. Psalm 33:18-19 says, "Watch this: God's eye is on those who respect him, the ones who are looking for his love. He's ready to come to their rescue in bad times; in lean times he keeps body and soul together." Seeing through the eyes of God means looking at and valuing His faithfulness. He always remains the same, infinitely exalted above change. Due to His unchangeableness, God lavishes goodness and mercy upon us each day. His faithfulness is based on His covenant promises, not on our limitations.

Do you want to expand your myopic outlook on life? Then become intentional about focusing on God's faithfulness. Remember that He watches your every move and that He will rescue you in troubled times. Waiting for God with this perspective will cause the blinders of fear and doubt to fall from your eyes like scales.

NOTHING ESCAPES GOD'S GAZE. WE ONLY SEE THE RISKS ASSOCIATED WITH A LONG DELAY OF OUR DESIRES, WHILE GOD SEES THE REWARDS.

I believe that David saw his giant through the eyes of God because of the way he responded to the challenge. He did not flinch or faint. He did not doubt or decline the opportunity to be active but expected God to do what He had done before. Even though David was not a part of Saul's army, no feeble excuses fell from his lips. God was watching, and David knew it. First Samuel 2:3 states, "For God knows what's going on. He takes the measure of everything that happens." Nothing escapes God's gaze. We only see the risks associated with a long delay of our desires, while God sees the rewards.

I believe that what we are determines what we see. Consequently, what we see determines what we do. Recently, I heard about a young boy named Alex whose story demonstrates this truth. The way he viewed himself and his circumstances played a major role in how he responded to his challenge.

Alex's mother was deaf and suffered from an incurable disease. The boy loved his mother very much, and he would do anything to please her. His mother asked that he learn to play the piano. So the boy took lessons for many years, but never seemed to excel. Each week, his teacher was disappointed by his performance and discouraged him from continuing, even though he practiced for hours each day. Alex was given the label, "musically challenged." Nevertheless, he continued to practice, if only to please his ailing mother. Every now and then, you could hear Alex say to his teacher, "Some day my mom is going to hear me play." It would be a long time before the teacher understood the significance of Alex's words.

One summer, as the annual student recital approached, the boy's teacher anticipated Alex's usual disappointing performance. He had consistently fumbled over and butchered selections by Brahms and Mozart for the past seven recitals. There was no reason for the teacher to expect anything different this time. She put him as the last performer on the program with the intention of salvaging the recital by playing a selection after him.

As the boy sat down at the Steinway, the teacher hoped against hope and took a deep breath. Much to her surprise, Alex selected Mozart's Concerto #21 in C major. For six minutes, the teacher watched with astonishment as Alex's hands swept across the keyboard. When he was done, the teacher knew that something unbelievable had occurred. Alex had played like a musical giant. It was an amazing performance, and the teacher was overwhelmed by what she had heard. The crowd rose quickly to their feet and gave the boy a long and resounding ovation.

Overcome by emotion, the teacher threw her arms around Alex and said, "I've never heard you play like that! How'd you do it?" The boy replied, "Remember when I told you that my mom was sick? Actually, she had cancer and passed away this morning. So tonight was the first time she ever heard me play." Alex envisioned his mom in heaven listening to him play. What this boy saw made a difference in what he did. Similarly, seeing things with God's faithfulness in view can transform even the most pathetic and pitiful people into giant-slayers.

FACING THE GIANTS IN YOUR LIFE

Problems are only opportunities in work clothes. Goliath-sized challenges in our relationships, our ministries, our careers or our finances can test our view of God's greatness. But when we face these issues head on, we often realize that they are not as insurmountable as we first thought.

Like most people, I tend to run from big challenges. It is easier to retreat than to face the possibility of defeat. But I have come to understand that running is a child's way of dealing with big issues. Problems never go away if you ignore them. Rather, they usually morph into bigger monsters or mushroom into a hard-to-manage mess.

At some point, you must acknowledge the need to confront. This was David's attitude, and this is what brings solutions. Start the way he did—by taking a stand for God. Stand for righteousness, mercy, grace and unselfishness. Stand for excellence, purity and unswerving compassion. I'm tired of the liberals always getting the credit for being compassionate and the conservatives and evangelicals getting the credit for being mean and insensitive. Stand for love, justice and truth. Stand for everything God represents. Don't compromise. Take a stand for God.

Even while he was waiting for God, David held on to his principles and beliefs. He stood on the truth that God was not to be taken lightly. This young man became so consumed with decimating the giant for the sake of God's reputation that he forgot about the potential danger to himself. He valued God's name more than his own reputation.

Facing down big issues will always result in an adjusting of our values. It means looking with compassion and mercy at a homeless man living under a bridge. It means looking without judgment at a 15-year-old unwed mother. It also means seeing the world as a harvest field instead of a place filled with hopelessness.

I recently heard the Lord whisper, "Every warrior has a battle to win, even while he waits for Me." I believe that this is a lesson for all of us. God was telling me that I am a *warrior in waiting* and that I must not take this season lying down. God does not want us to walk around like whimpering little puppies. He has given us the weapons to win the waiting game. The Bible says that "it is not by sword or spear that the Lord saves; for the battle is the Lord's" (1 Sam. 17:47, *NIV*).

When battling or confronting giant challenges in our marriage, on the job, or in any other area of life, we need to stand in faith, because God is on our side. The Spirit of God will lead and direct our steps. God is a sharpshooter, and if we follow Him, we'll eventually hit our target with great impact.

Taking a stand for God also means realizing that we are confronting problems and not necessarily people. We must strive to uphold the dignity of God in a godless society, instead of only protecting our own interests and reputation. We are seeking to reflect a godly character. I believe that this attitude will help us maintain the right perspective and a right response in the midst of our battles.

Keep in mind that righteous confrontation leads to intimacy in relationships, productivity in responsibilities, and peace regarding the things that we cannot change. In the past, I confronted problems by dwelling on how I was being mistreated. I spent my time dwelling on all of the negative things that could happen to me if the situations in my life did not change. Finally, after stewing in my own bitter juices, I proceeded to deliver judgments (mine, not God's) on those who had offended me.

I now realize that godly confrontation is the key to restoration. Today, I follow a different set of steps. First, I acknowledge my own shortcomings and ask for God's forgiveness. One old lady used to say, "Honey, you better go and smell yourself," referring to people who needed to make an attitude adjustment. What she meant by this statement is that self-examination is a necessary part of being in right relationship with God and with others. Second, I do my best to humbly confront others—being quick to listen, quick to forgive, and open to compromise. The Bible admonishes us to "make every effort to live in peace with all men" (Heb. 12:14, *NIV*). And third, I work at taking responsibility for my emotions. No one can *make* me mad, sad or glad. My emotional state is *my own* responsibility. No matter what happens to me, I alone choose my response and disposition.

Taking these three steps has helped me to resolve issues and salvage relationships while waiting for God. Today, I am free to better serve the Lord and others, and there is a greater consistency in my character in this walk of faith.

CLEAN OUT YOUR CLOSET

Often, the giants we face are not big, brutish beasts with bronze helmets and spears. They are sometimes inner struggles—secret, silent, sinful and invisible. In some ways, these inner giants are more difficult to defeat than a physical Goliath. Still, each giant must be defeated during our time in the waiting room.

I have found that those who are waiting for God tend to waste a lot of time storing baggage in their emotional closets. We pack our hurts, deep disappointments and pain away from the eyes of the world. Yet we privately coddle self-pity, discouragement, jealousy, envy, doubt in God, doubt in ourselves and, most deadly of all, regret. Regret keeps us looking back at lost time, mistakes and offenses. Ultimately, each of these things we secretly hold on to prevent us from looking forward. Periodically, we need to get rid of this old baggage.

Now and then when I am joking with friends, I'll sometimes tell someone in the group, "You need *professional* help." Although we laugh about it and continue on with our conversation, we each know that a little expert spiritual advice from a Bible-believing, reputable counselor is something everyone can use from time to time. I know a woman who has benefited from seeing a Christian counselor and who as a result is planning to write a book titled *Things My Therapist Told Me*.

I recognize that visiting a mental health professional is looked down on in some Christian circles. Yet the Bible is replete with the command to seek counsel in times of confusion or trouble. Proverbs 15:22 says, "Plans fail for lack of counsel, but with many advisers they succeed" (*NIV*). The woman I am referring to says that seeing her therapist is a great source of cathartic relief—especially in those times when she can't seem to pray her way through a problem. She says, "After our session is over, my spiritual closet is cleaner and I am more in touch with the truth that sets me free." This freedom makes it easy for her to line up with God's timing for her life.

Talking through issues helps us to unpack psychological baggage and to take out our emotional garbage, confirming the truth found in James 5:16, "Make this your common practice: Confess your sins to each other and pray for each other so that you can live together whole and healed."

TAKE A RISK AND REAP THE REWARDS

Whenever we're in the center of a divine delay, Goliath-sized challenges tend to rear their ugly heads. God wants to equip us to handle every challenge that comes our way. But we must be willing to take a risk. The risk is not in doing something foolish or dangerous. The risk is daring to do something great for the cause of God.

Right now, I am in the midst of taking a risk for the cause of God by making a major shift in my ministry. In some ways, I feel like a ship out at sea without a sail. Still, I know that it is the right time for the change and that I'm doing the right thing. But I have no revelation on exactly how things will turn out. I love what author and teacher John Piper has to say about taking a risk for the cause of God:

> We are not God. We do not know about tomorrow. And therefore risk is built right into the fabric of our finite lives. You can't avoid risk even if you want to. Ignorance

GOD WANTS TO EQUIP US TO HANDLE EVERY CHALLENGE THAT COMES OUR WAY. BUT WE MUST BE WILLING TO TAKE A RISK.

and uncertainty about tomorrow is our native air. All of
our plans for tomorrow's activities can be shattered by a
thousand unknowns whether we stay at home under the
covers or whether we ride the freeways.[1]

I believe that risk-taking is essential for survival. When we're
facing a Goliath-sized problem, it may not be safe to choose the
comfort of security when something great may be achieved for
the cause of God and the good of others.

"Are you caught in the enchantment of security, paralyzed
from taking any risks for the cause of God? Or have you been
freed by the power of the Holy Spirit from the mirage of . . .
worldly safety and comfort?"[2] Do you ever say with David, "The
LORD has rescued me from the claws of lions and bears, and he
will keep me safe from the hands of this Philistine" (1 Sam.
17:37, CEV). David took a strategic risk for the cause of God and
left the outcome up to Him. He had no special revelation from
God on this issue. He had to make a decision on the basis of
God's track record of faithfulness. So, he made his decision to
act and trusted the results to God. The risk paid off.

We can't run away when we are faced with a formidable risk
during our divine delay. Warriors don't retreat. They face
tough times head on with an attitude of sobriety and boldness.
We need to take a risk by trusting in a God who is bigger than
the biggest obstacle we will ever face. Does this mean that
everyone who takes a risk for the cause of God will end up on
top? No, it does not. There is no promise that every effort for
the cause of God will succeed, at least not in the short-term.

WE ARE ON A TEMPORARY ASSIGNMENT

Another reason we should take a risk is because, after all, this life
is only a temporary assignment. As a long shot in God's slingshot,

we need to see that our present assignment is a prelude to God's next assignment. All of our assignments here on Earth are temporary, because one day we'll spend eternity in heaven completing our permanent mission—to worship God forever and ever.

David's first job was as a shepherd boy. Later, God strategically positioned him to become a giant-slayer. But notice a key principle: In the eyes of God, assignments are handed out privately before they are made public. Like David, we must first work behind the scenes before we can go center stage. Earthly assignments are sometimes designed to teach us about God. Later, they position us to reach others *for* God.

The Bible says that while David was shepherding in the fields, he killed a lion and a bear to protect his earthly father's sheep. Later, on the battlefield, David killed the giant Goliath in order to protect his heavenly Father's sheep—the children of Israel. This is a wonderful picture that helps us see things through God's eyes. Our present assignment is serving as a teacher, preparing us to make a greater impact on the world.

David's turning point came because he did not regard himself as a small fish in a big pond. David did not rely on false humility, nor did he see his lack of battleground experience as a handicap. His faith was not disabled by self-doubt. Rather, he relied on his past experiences with God to launch him from the shepherd's field to the battlefield. Similarly, our past victories, no matter how small, should act as a springboard that propels us into the future.

Look at what David told King Saul just before he went in for the kill: "Master . . . don't give up hope. I'm ready to go and fight this Philistine" (1 Sam. 17:32). Saul answered David, "You can't go and fight this Philistine. You're too young and inexperienced—and he's been at this fighting business since before you were born" (v. 33). In graphic detail, David then read his resume:

I've been a shepherd, tending sheep for my father. Whenever a lion or bear came and took a lamb from the flock, I'd go after it, knock it down, and rescue the lamb. If it turned on me, I'd grab it by the throat, wring its neck, and kill it. Lion or bear, it made no difference— I killed it. And I'll do the same to this Philistine pig who is taunting the troops of God-Alive. God, who delivered me from the teeth of the lion and the claws of the bear, will deliver me from this Philistine (vv. 34-37).

How can we cultivate the kind of perspective that recognizes our temporary assignment as helpful and not hurtful? The turning point comes when we do what David did—when we reach back and hold on to the graphic images of our past victories in God. Like David, we also have a resume of God's power working in our life. These images act as our rocks and the slingshot, aimed at any giant that comes our way. No matter the size of our experiences, God can use them to create something great out of something ordinary.

A friend recently shared with me these sayings about the mentality of someone who has put their trust in God's ability to create purpose out of any situation:

- Some bread and fish in my hands is a fish and chips meal for one. But in God's hands, it feeds 5,000 people. It all depends on whose hands it is in!

- A rock in my hand is a skip across the water. But in David's hand, it can bring down a giant. It all depends on whose hand it's in!

- A rod in my hand can chase a big dog. But in Moses' hand, it can open the Red Sea. It all depends on whose hand it's in!

• Some spit and mud in my hand is just a dirty mess. But in Jesus' hand, it is new eyes for the blind. It all depends on whose hand it's in!

• A nail in my hand is an amateur attempt at carpentry. But in Jesus' hands, it's life for the world. It all depends on whose hand it's in!

• A few dollars in my hand won't go very far. But in Jesus' hands, it becomes a seed that can yield thirty-, sixty- and a hundredfold. It all depends on whose hand it's in!

Notice how these truths unveil God's divine ways. He miraculously uses the past to position us for the present. Look at how God takes the weak people of this world and uses them to amaze the strong. Note how He takes the lowly and raises them up to places of authority. He lifts up those who have been put down. Long shots typically face enormous odds. But it is the existence of those gigantic odds that will prove God's supreme power to accomplish the impossible.

YOU HAVE A HIDDEN ADVANTAGE

Every long shot has hidden advantages—abilities that can't be seen with the naked eye. This is why hidden advantages are so dangerous. Our hidden advantage is God's help and protection while we wait for Him. Hope makes us a force to be reckoned with. Hope is an expectation of a future reward for something beyond our own power to attain.

If you are like me, every time God delays a promised blessing, you are drawn to hope more than ever before. But, if we're honest, we are sometimes tempted to depend on other things as well. I start by leaning on my own ingenuity, my friends, my family or my money. These things are tangible, while hope seems so nebulous. They can be manipulated, but God cannot. I can't see hope with my eyes. I can't feel it with my hands or taste it with my mouth. So I struggle to get my arms around this unseen advantage. In order for me to have hope in God, I must learn to be childlike in my expectations of Him. Childlike hope is a carefree assurance of divine assistance.

Have you ever watched a father cautiously, but playfully, toss his baby daughter into the air? As she floats up through the atmosphere and back down into his arms, a happy carefree smile washes over her baby-smooth face. Her expectation of a safe landing is strong because she knows that in her father's care, she is safe and secure. "We wait in hope for the LORD; he is our help and shield" (Ps. 33:20, *NIV*). When we are waiting for God, we must depend on Him and Him alone. He has everything we need.

Yet even if we fall or fail in some way, God's mercy and sovereignty is still at work, positioning us to have an impact on the lives of others. Our hidden hurts may be the hidden advantage that He'll put to use at some future time. Not long ago, one of my protégés came to me during such a season in her life.

Shannon is a slender, petite woman, filled with a fire that can never be doused by the obstacles of life. What she lacks in physical height she makes up for with her zeal for God. Whenever someone challenges the character of God, Shannon stands tall to defend His reputation. She is a tiger in disguise.

In 2000, the gentle nudging of the Holy Spirit prompted Shannon to return to school for a master's degree in Christian counseling. Soon the time came for her to begin an internship at a rehab facility. Although Shannon was accustomed to dealing with people recovering from the devastating emotional and physical impact of drugs, nothing could have prepared her for what lay ahead. The spiritual atmosphere at the rehab facility was the most oppressive environment she had ever experienced.

Depression, anxiety and obsessive, controlling and manipulating spirits permeated the place. Shannon later learned someone had recently committed suicide at the site. Although the rehab facility allowed the residents to trust in a higher power, they were not permitted to say the name of Jesus. Shannon wondered why they had selected her to become a counselor, since she was studying at a seminary.

In no way did Shannon break any of their rules. She ran support group meetings, conducted drug tests, and handled administrative tasks. Her conversations with the directors were always cordial, and they were very receptive to her concerns. Near the end of her internship, she was told that her supervisor would be visiting to discuss the possibility of recruiting additional interns from her school. The day came and she was ushered into the directors' office. Shannon was shocked when they accused her of being reluctant to accept the philosophy and treatment milieu at the rehab. This tiger in disguise was uncharacteristically speechless—unable to defend herself. Her supervisor didn't ask the directors for clarity, nor did she employ the required standard evaluation format to assess Shannon's alleged inability to meet the facility's standards.

Shannon relayed the story to me saying, "I left the rehab within an hour after the meeting. I felt stunned, deceived, manipulated and betrayed by my supervisor." Then she told me that inwardly she questioned why she had not stood up for herself. She wondered whether she could continue on at the rehab facility.

During a meeting one day with a prayer leader from our church, God showed Shannon something surprising. She was unaware that the accusations had wounded her deeply and silenced the tiger that was down inside of her. Shannon said, "The prayer leader told me to close my eyes and meditate on a particular passage of Scripture. Within seconds, I had a memory of my father during a physically abusive episode that occurred when I was in my early teens. I began to weep. Then I heard the voice of the Holy Spirit say that He had protected me, and that although I had come to believe that I could never do anything right, it was a lie."

Shannon confessed that she had been harboring this unhealed wound that had been inflicted by her father. That day, she released her father from the prison of unforgiveness that she had created for him deep in her heart. Two months later, her father passed away. Shannon knew that she had experienced a sequence of events that were divinely orchestrated by God. She was made whole concerning her relationship with her dad and was now prepared to be a better counselor.

In June of the following year, Shannon began an internship at a faith-based rehab center for men. The atmosphere was warm and encouraging. Chapel services and Bible study were the norm, not the exception. Prayer was offered at the beginning and end of all group sessions, and men were finding freedom from their past addictions.

In hindsight, the delay proved to be strategic. The tiger was back, and her impact was greater than ever. Expect God's purposes to be at work in you even while waiting for Him. At the appointed time, like Shannon you'll be propelled like a rock from His slingshot—affecting the lives of others in the process.

SURVIVAL SECRETS
Remember

The Picture from the Past: By confronting your Goliath-sized problems, you'll position yourself for a glimpse of God's greatness working in you and for you.

The Practice for the Present: You need to see issues through God's eyes. When you adjust your values, you'll adjust your vision.

The Promise for the Future: "God, who delivered me from the teeth of the lion and the claws of the bear, will deliver me from this Philistine" (1 Sam. 17:37).

Notes
1. John Piper, "Risk and the Cause of God," sermon delivered April 26, 1987. http://www.desiringgod.org/library/sermons/87/042687.html.
2. John Piper, *Don't Waste Your Life* (Wheaton, IL: Crossway Books, 2003).

CHAPTER FIVE

What in the World Is God Waiting For?

GOD COULD CHANGE THE WORLD HIMSELF,
BUT HE WAITS TO DO IT THROUGH YOU.

When we're in the midst of a divine delay, it's natural to wonder about what God is waiting for. Since God doesn't always share with us the reason for the delay, our patience is often reduced to the point where our musings become more agitated and we ask in frustration, "What in the *world* is God waiting for?"

I believe that one answer is that God is waiting to give us a great return on our investment. I'm not referring to financial investment, but to a type of investment that's important to God. When our lives are characterized by prayer, giving, caring for people, working in ministry, being an excellent employee, or serving our community, we are making rich investments in the lives of those around us. As a result, we'll take away great returns. God will entrust us with greater success, more responsibilities and increased influence when we make serving the needs of others a priority.

Life really is all about investments and returns. On the surface, our investments in the lives of others may seem unappreciated, unnoticed, mundane and even insignificant. But, on a much deeper level, we're doing the same kinds of things that Jesus did—changing lives one moment at a time and one person at a time. God could certainly change the world all by Himself, but He waits to do it through us. He keeps us where we are so that we're used to the fullest extent possible before moving us on to our next assignment. Once this has been accomplished, we'll inevitably be rewarded for a life well lived. A life well lived is one in which we diligently do the things we already know to do—the things Jesus revealed to us through His example while He was here on Earth.

There are some things that God conceals from us (for a time), and then there are things that He openly reveals. In various areas of our life, God has clearly shown us what to do though the Scriptures, through prayer, through godly counsel, or through the ministry of the Holy Spirit. For example, my assignment during this season in my life is to serve as a pastor, musician, administrator, leader, wife and parent of two teenagers. While I am called to do other things—and though there are deep yearnings in my heart to accomplish more—I must first accomplish the things that I know to do today.

We need to avoid becoming obsessed with the future and the things that God has concealed from us and instead strive to become consumed with what He has revealed. Otherwise, we may miss the significance of our current season by failing to invest our life's energies wisely. We must be careful about throwing away our vocation, our ministry, our relationships or anything that may seem fruitless and frustrating at this time.

Sadly, most people live in a "Wish I" world in which they would rather be someone else or live somewhere else. Yet we can take advantage of this season and maximize our returns by doing what we know to do. King Solomon said, "Whatever your hand finds to do, do it with all your might, for in the grave, where you are going, there is neither working nor planning nor knowledge nor wisdom" (Eccles. 9:10, *NIV*).

REALIZE THE SIGNIFICANCE OF THIS SEASON

When I was growing up, my mom and dad sometimes left my three brothers and me home alone. We were expected to take good care of the house while we waited for them to return. On one particular day while my parents were out, my youngest brother decided to playfully hit his head against the large fish tank in our living room. And just as responsible, caring siblings should, the rest of us stood by and watched, waiting for the inevitable disaster to occur. Sure enough, after several taps of his noggin against the side of the tank, the glass shattered. The water from the tank gushed through the cracks and the gold fish poured onto the floor. Needless to say, Mom and Dad knew that we were not ready for greater responsibility. We did not understand the significance of that current season, when responsibility had been entrusted to us.

Jesus told a story about three servants who were given the responsibility of investing varying amounts of wealth while their master went away on a long journey. As they waited for his return, the servants were supposed to maximize their own season of great responsibility. In the story, all three servants accepted the responsibility and waited for their master to return. However, only two of the servants waited wisely, while the other did not.

The first two servants invested their master's wealth, and their ventures yielded a great return. When their master returned, they were rewarded with greater responsibility and an affirmation of, "Well done, good and faithful servant! You have been faithful with a few things; I will put you in charge of many things" (Matt. 25:21, *NIV*). The third servant, who had been entrusted with the smallest amount of wealth, wasted his opportunity by digging a hole and placing his treasure in the ground. He was not rewarded for burying his treasure, but punished for his foolishness. Matthew recounts the conversation between this servant and his master:

> "Sir, I know that you are hard to get along with. You harvest what you don't plant and gather crops where you haven't scattered seed. I was frightened and went out and hid your money in the ground. Here is every single coin!" The master of the servant told him, "You are lazy and good-for-nothing! You know that I harvest what I don't plant and gather crops where I haven't scattered seed. You could have at least put my money in the bank, so that I could have earned interest on it" (Matt. 25:24-27, *CEV*).

This pitiful servant gave a pitiful excuse and blamed his lack of productivity on his master's tough standards. What he was actually saying was, "Boss, I didn't think that I could please you." But in reality, he never took the time to learn how to please his master. He never learned how his master became so wealthy and successful. Perhaps somewhere down deep in his lazy little soul, he expected the master to always treat him like a servant. However, by this time, the master was willing to treat him like a steward.

If the servant had understood the significance of this season and that his master was waiting to give him a great return on his investments, I'm sure that he would have looked at his opportunities very differently. He would have been a much wiser investor. Sadly, the only thing the lazy servant focused on was watching the master with fear and awe. We need to have a deep sense of reverence for God, but that should not stop us from boldly and lavishly living for Him.

Obviously, the master could have invested the wealth him-self. Yet he went away, waited, and allowed his servants to do it for him. Why did he do that? What in the world was the master thinking? Well, among other things, I believe that he wanted to teach his servants the importance of living their lives based on a pattern. The master in this parable symbolized God, so the pattern being portrayed was none other than God's plan of how we should wisely invest our life's energies and resources. It is through this kind of living that we become spiritually strong and mature servants, ready to fulfill God's plan for mankind.

As we follow God's pattern, we learn to wait and to be responsible for the important things left in our care. Jesus said, "Walk with me and work with me—watch how I do it. Learn the unforced rhythms of grace. I won't lay anything heavy or ill-fitting on you. Keep company with me and you'll learn to live freely and lightly" (Matt. 11:29-30).

It is essential that we understand the way God works while we wait for Him. It is vitally important for us to realize that this is not a time to be afraid of God or a time to play games. It's a time to occupy until He comes. God waits so that He can increase our returns and give our best to the people around us. But He will not wait forever. And when He returns, He'll confront us with His expectation.

What kind of increase will you have? What kind of reward can you expect?

AS WE FOLLOW GOD'S PATTERN, WE LEARN TO WAIT AND TO BE RESPONSIBLE FOR THE IMPORTANT THINGS LEFT IN OUR CARE.

MAKE SERVICE YOUR PRIORITY

One of the most effective ways to change the world is to serve the needs of the world. Isn't that what Jesus did? Although He was mistreated and misunderstood, He helped us when we did not even realize we needed it. When we needed a way to the Father, Jesus came and served us so that we might have it. When we needed truth, Jesus became truth in the flesh. When we needed life, Jesus gave His precious blood for ours. Jesus became the perfect servant in order to meet the needs of mankind. And when He was done, He transitioned to His ultimate position next to the Father in heaven. Our service to others is not time wasted; it is time invested for the future. The extent to which we will change the lives of others is the extent to which our lives will be also be changed.

For a long time, I have been intrigued by the story of Zechariah and Elizabeth, the elderly parents of John the Baptist. Zechariah and Elizabeth were childless until the birth of their only son, and they must have been puzzled about why their prayers went unanswered for so long. The Jewish people considered children to be a sign of God's favor. Childlessness was considered to be a mark of His disapproval. But this could not have been the case with Zechariah and Elizabeth, for the Bible says that they were blameless in God's sight (see Luke 1:6).

Yet Zechariah and Elizabeth's barrenness was not the focus of their lives. Even though they were old and seemingly dried up, they were not idle as they waited. They were determined to have a fulfilling life of service despite the socially and emotionally crippling effects of barrenness. Service is what they lived for, and their service paid off with unexpected benefits.

One day, an angel of the Lord appeared to Zechariah when he was on duty serving as a priest before God. When Zechariah saw the angel, he was startled and gripped with fear. But the angel said:

Do not be afraid, Zechariah; your prayer has been heard. Your wife Elizabeth will bear you a son, and you are to give him the name John. He will be a joy and delight to you, and many will rejoice because of his birth, for he will be great in the sight of the Lord. . . . And he will go on before the Lord, in the spirit and power of Elijah, to turn the hearts of the fathers to their children and the disobedient to the wisdom of the righteous—to make ready a people prepared for the Lord (Luke 1:12-17, NIV).

The Bible goes on to say that when Zechariah's time of service was completed, he returned home. Soon after this, Elizabeth became pregnant. As her days of delay were almost over, she was overwhelmed by the goodness of God, and declared, "The Lord has done this for me. . . . In these days he has shown his favor and taken away my disgrace among the people" (Luke 1:25, NIV). Through these miraculous events, John the Baptist was born. His dramatic arrival was significant in God's divine design.

This story parallels a similar account of Abraham and Sarah in the book of Genesis. Both of these accounts beautifully reveal that there is a purpose in our waiting. John's life and ministry prepared the way for Christ. It also had a powerful impact on the welfare and destiny of the people around him. His message had prophetic significance, because through it God foretold some important news concerning the future of the nation of Israel. Zechariah and Elizabeth's long-awaited pregnancy also prepared them for the even greater responsibility of protecting and mentoring Mary, the mother of Jesus, during the first few months of her pregnancy. All of these things happened in the midst of their service to others.

God is not looking for those who do just enough to get by. Rather, the measure of our service determines the measure of our reward. Our earthly and eternal returns will not be calculated in monetary gains but in changed lives. And we may never know the magnitude of our contribution to another's life until we meet that person in eternity.

INDIVIDUAL SERVICE BUILDS A CARING COMMUNITY

Making service a priority is not always easy—especially when it means serving in a community. Our families, churches and workplaces are what I call "micro-communities." Serving in a micro-community with people we know and with people who know us is often the hardest place to invest our time and energies. But our perspective can change when we realize how much the survival of others depends on our contribution. Without us, what would happen to our family? Without us, what would happen to the people we lead or serve at work? What would the people in our church do if we simply dropped out of sight?

Every community is made up of a group of people tied together by a common bond and cooperating for a common purpose. Yet there is an element of individual sacrifice involved in serving the needs of the people with whom we live and work.

The documentary *March of the Penguins* follows the emperor penguins of Antarctica as they embark on an incredible journey through ice and snow to mating grounds 70 miles inland. Narrated by Morgan Freeman, this beautiful film captures the drama of these three-foot-high birds in the most inhospitable environment.

Once the males reach the breeding grounds, they are given responsibility for the eggs. For a while, their competitive nature is overridden for the sake of survival. When a massive storm sets in and vicious winds begin to pelt the penguins, they respond by huddling together in a single mass. As the view alternates from

close-ups of ice-caked penguins to panoramic shots of the hud-
dled throng, Freeman narrates:

> As the fathers settle into their long wait at the breeding
> grounds, the temperature is now 80 degrees below zero.
> That's without taking into account the wind, which can
> blow 100 miles per hour. Though they can be aggressive
> during the rest of the year, at this time the males are
> totally docile, a united and cooperative team. They brace
> against the storm by merging their thousand bodies into
> a single mass. They will take turns, each of them getting
> to spend some time near the center of their huddle
> where it's warmer.[1]

Individually, the penguins would have frozen to death, but
together there was a degree of warmth that could only be pro-
duced in community. What does all this have to do with waiting
for God? God uses groups of waiting, self-sacrificing people to
encourage and sustain each other. This is how God works during divine delays. Remember how the disciples waited together
in the upper room for the comfort and power of the Holy Spirit?
We're all waiting for God to come through for us in some way or
another. So why not serve one another while we wait? Through
the power of the Spirit, we'll find a special measure of grace as we
engage in serving those around us.

Service is God's way of making us great. Dr. Paul Rees said,
"If you want a picture of success as heaven measures it, of greatness as God views it, don't look for the blaring of the bands on
Broadway; listen, rather, for the tinkle of water splashing into a
basin, while God incarnate, in a humility that makes angels hold
their breaths, sponges the grime from the feet of His undeserv-
ing disciples."[2] Over the years, I have learned to invest in the lives
of the people in three simple ways:

1. *Spend time building strong relationships or repairing neglected relationships.* How many of our friends and family members have been on our things-to-do list, people-to-call list, or people-to-take-out-to-lunch list? Waiting seasons are the days to get out of the doghouse with the ones we care about. We can start by establishing a regular time of fellowship and opening lines of communication.

2. *Mentor others by showing how we overcame some of the same challenges they're presently experiencing.* Most of us are so consumed with our own issues that often we don't realize the great truths we've learned about God and life. Others can benefit from our life story.

3. *Speak positively about life.* I believe that people around us are influenced by the words we speak. If we are negative about life, we're likely spreading a poisonous perspective of the value of our time and tearing down the hope of others for a better tomorrow. Most people are waiting for God to do something in their lives. We can become a great source of faith by making our communication with others a wellspring of hope concerning God's unfailing help. Psalm 33:20 should be our basis: "We wait in hope for the Lord; he is our help and our shield"(*NIV*).

HOLD ON TO BLAMELESSNESS

"Both of them were upright in the sight of God, observing all the Lord's commandments and regulations blamelessly" (Luke 1:6, *NIV*). What a beautiful testimony Zechariah and Elizabeth had. I wish this could be said of us all. But why wait until we're old?

Wherever we find ourselves in this journey, we need to invest in the task of developing blamelessness. But it won't happen unless we seek and carefully strive for this all-important goal. Living a blameless life is obtainable, no matter how restricting our circumstances might be.

Achieving blamelessness is not as hard as you might think, because blamelessness is not sinlessness. The Bible does not say that Zech and Liz were sinless. Sinlessness is impossible, for we have all sinned and will continue to sin, although unintentionally. Blamelessness simply means "a total allegiance to God accompanied by living in the conscious awareness of His presence in all aspects of life."[3] It means having a clear conscience. *THE MESSAGE* puts it this way: "Together they lived honorably before God, careful in keeping to the ways of the commandments and enjoying a clear conscience before God. But they were childless because Elizabeth could never conceive, and now they were quite old" (Luke 1:6-7).

So it really is possible to be barren and blameless at the same time. We really can be in good standing with God yet frustrated and fruitless in some major aspect of life. For me, the revelation of this truth was a great awakening (and the genesis of this book). For many years, I strived to live honorably before God and was careful to be obedient to Him. By God's grace, I had accomplished many significant things. Yet I still felt that there was more for me to do. I worked hard and wondered when my efforts would produce greater fruitfulness. Knowing that one

IT REALLY IS POSSIBLE TO BE BARREN AND BLAMELESS AT THE SAME TIME. WE CAN BE IN GOOD STANDING WITH GOD YET FRUSTRATED AND FRUITLESS IN SOME ASPECT OF LIFE.

can be blameless but still barren lifted a weight of false guilt off of my shoulders, and I settled into a whole new dimension of love and service to the Lord.

Through this revelation, I learned that a clear conscience is absolutely essential to successfully waiting for God. Without it, many people struggle with the disease of false guilt. This occurs when a person feels guilty without actually committing a violation. In his book *A Doctor's Casebook in the Light of the Bible,* Dr. Paul Tournier, a noted Christian physician, writes, "False guilt is that which comes as a result of judgments and suggestions of men. True guilt is that which results from divine judgment."[4]

God causes us to feel legitimate remorse to awaken our conscience when we act irresponsibly. Christians call this *conviction,* and it alerts us to specific actions and thoughts that go against God's standard for our lives. False guilt is Satan's way of making us think that our situation is the result of some kind of shortcoming in our life. This emotion causes our mind and heart to become a ball of stress that robs us of joy and peace. Anyone who lives with this kind of mind-set needs to know that the joy of blamelessness comes when we do what Zechariah and Elizabeth did: avoid false guilt and acknowledge God's sovereignty.

Not long ago, I experienced a bout with false guilt in a way that I had never known before. It was as if a part of me had secretly slipped into eternity while no one was watching. Today, I still wonder how I was so unaware of the shift happening deep inside of me. It occurred when I experienced my second miscarriage in two years. One night, I simply got out of bed to use the bathroom and suddenly found myself in shock and disbelief as I held in my hands the fragmented form of a 12-week-old fetus. Even though the pregnancy had been labeled "high risk," I was unprepared for the loss.

Before my baby was given even a chance to breathe, his life was gone like a vapor. I would never hear his cry. I would never hold his hand. David and I went to the hospital, gripped by all kinds of uncertainties. We wanted to be wrong, but we were not. With the news that the pregnancy was over, we embraced and wept together. Our only comfort was in knowing that heaven had called our little one home and that someday we would see his face.

In the following weeks, I prayed for God's peace. Yet my mind was filled with all kinds of questions. The biggest one was, *Lord, why now?* I was convinced that God's timing was all wrong. The pregnancy had been unplanned—I was no spring chicken, and the idea of being a new mother at my age took some getting used to. Yet just hours before the miscarriage occurred, my heart had settled into a place of peace and excitement about having another child. In the end, I was baffled about the timing of both—the pregnancy and the loss.

In the absence of any real answers, I blamed myself for not coming to terms with the pregnancy sooner. I felt that somehow the miscarriage was my fault. But as I spent time worshiping God, the guilt slowly gave way to the comforting presence of the Holy Spirit.

I came to realize that along with God's sovereignty, we live in a world in which Satan's power has not yet been totally defeated. As Bill Hybels puts it:

Unspeakable tragedies afflict believers and nonbelievers alike. The righteous suffer and the innocent perish. Unsuspecting worshipers are killed without cause; a tower topples onto eighteen Jews, crushing them indiscriminately (Luke 13:1-4). The apostle James is beheaded while Peter is miraculously delivered (Acts 12). The apostle Paul suffers all his life from a thorn in the flesh and finally dies under the ax of the Roman executioner. Many Christians sense that God hears and empathizes with their prayers, but some requests remain unanswered.

Why would an all-loving, all-powerful God deny valid requests from faithful believers?

It's important to remember that despite the victory God has achieved over Satan in the ministry and resurrection of Christ, all things are not yet submitted to God. The enemy is still active. And although his years are counted and his end is sure, he still remains the prince of this world and oppresses the ways of God. He causes much suffering, and often seems to have the upper hand. Because of this ultimate victory, Christians have the assurance that those very prayers, which remained unanswered in this life, will receive spectacular vindication in eternity.[5]

We need to hold on to the truth that there is no sin or shame in being barren when we live blamelessly before God. Time and His sovereignty will win out over our present emptiness.

DISCOVER GOD IN THE DETAILS OF LIFE

Spiritual things happen in the midst of the ordinary and the necessary details of life. Oswald Chambers wrote, "We can all see God in exceptional things, but it requires the culture of spiritual discipline to see God in every detail. Never allow that the haphazard is anything less than God's appointed order, and be ready to discover the divine designs anywhere."[6]

On the day that Zechariah went to the Temple, he did not know that God was at work in the mundane details of his time of service. Zechariah stepped once again into the Temple to attend to his normal responsibilities. He was just an unsuspecting soul, and unprepared for an encounter with the unseen God. He was simply giving his time to perform simple tasks and was not doing anything out of the ordinary.

The problem with making the needs of others a priority is that we tend to believe that we're not really doing anything great. We want to do the things that rate high on our culture's success meter. We want our titles to be noticeable, our destinies to be paved with bright lights, and our Lord working for us with sirens blaring. Why must our spiritual lives be so shallow?

The great hindrance in spiritual life is that we will look for big things to do. Remember that Jesus took a towel and washed the disciples' feet. Deep, meaningful and, most of all, spiritual things happen when we're least expecting it. It's like the woman who had a little slogan over her kitchen sink that read, "Divine service is conducted here three times daily."

God is not intimidated by our demands for grand expressions of His Spirit here on Earth. But do those displays necessarily make us more aware of His presence and power? Can't spirituality and God's work be found in a staff meeting or in a well-run organization? Can't God's work be found in the midst of people who open a new restaurant? I believe that God works through the typical as well as the unusual. God works in the minds of those who sit down to come up with budgets for a new outreach center or to those who make plans for a new treatment center in the inner city. No matter how routine life may sometimes seem, we should remain alert to the beauty of God in the mundane things in life. The psalmist asks, "Who out there has a lust for life? Can't wait each day to come upon beauty?" (Ps. 34:12).

If we look hard enough, we will find God at work when we do the laundry, conduct business transactions, build buildings, and change diapers. And in the midst of these routine tasks, we don't need to know how God is working on a moment-by-moment basis.

One of the wisest statements that I ever heard about God being in the details of life was made by an old preacher who said,

"Often we'd all like a sign from God that the waiting will render a great reward. And sometimes those signs come. But even when there is no natural sign, the sign of the cross remains. If God could be, and indeed was, active in that most terrible of moments, then we are assured over and over again that there is no moment in our lives when God cannot be active. Add that to Jesus' promise never to leave us, and suddenly the mundane details of life shine with new meaning."

SURVIVAL SECRETS
Remember

The Picture from the Past: You really can be in right standing with God yet be frustrated and fruitless in some major aspect of life (see Luke 1:6-7).

The Practice for the Present: You need to avoid becoming obsessed with the future and the things God has concealed from you. Instead, strive to become enthusiastic about the tasks He has revealed. "Whatever your hand finds to do, do it with all your might, for in the grave, where you are going, there is neither working nor planning nor knowledge nor wisdom" (Eccles. 9:10, *NIV*).

The Promise for the Future: God waits to give you a great return on your investment.

Notes
1. "March of the Penguins: Community Guards Our Lives," Preaching Today.com, January 2006. http://www.christianitytoday.com/lyris/wiu/archives/01-09-2006.html.
2. Paul Lee Tan, *Encyclopedia of 7,700 Illustrations* (Garland, TX: Bible Communications, Inc., 1996), Logos Bible Software CD-ROM.
3. Alex Varughese, ed, *Discovering the Old Testament* (Kansas City, MO: Beacon Hill Press, 2003).

4. Paul Tournier, *A Doctor's Casebook in the Light of the Bible* (Godalming, UK: Highland Books, 1988).
5. Bill Hybels, *Too Busy Not to Pray* (Downers Grove, IL: InterVarsity Press, 1998).
6. Oswald Chambers, *My Utmost for His Highest* (Grand Rapids, MI: Discovery House Publishers, 1989).

CHAPTER SIX

Staying in Step with God

KEEP IN STEP WITH GOD'S LOVE, AS YOU
WAIT FOR OUR LORD JESUS CHRIST
TO SHOW HOW KIND HE IS BY GIVING
YOU ETERNAL LIFE.
JUDE 1:21, *CEV*

Right now, while you're in this waiting season, God wants to take you on a fantastic spiritual journey. Going on a journey while you are waiting may seem like an oxymoron, but it really is possible. In this period, you can travel to a fresh spiritual place and encounter intimacy in God's awesome presence. But there's one catch: You must stay in step with Him.

I'd like to briefly describe what staying in step with God looks like from Jesus' perspective. One day, our Savior had one of those, shall I say, tough talks with His friends. He said, "Anyone who intends to come with me has to let me lead. You're not in the driver's seat; I am. Don't run from suffering; embrace it. Follow me and I'll show you how" (Mark 8:34-35).

Simply stated, this means that staying in step with God is a moment-by-moment undertaking of following the example that Christ has set for you. It means allowing, again and again, the Holy Spirit to take up residence in the midst of your desires, actions and reactions. It means thinking, over and over again, the way Jesus thought, living the way He lived, and praying the way He prayed.

You may be surprised to know that staying in step with God comes through these simple repetitive actions. I'm not at all suggesting that you become a fanatic. You simply need to do the kinds of things that fill your heart and life with the fragrance of God on a consistent basis. So, if the waiting period you are in is threatening to slow your spiritual walk down to a crawl, don't take off your running shoes just yet. Constancy is the key to deeper spirituality.

FOLLOWING A GREAT EXAMPLE

Most people would agree that human beings are terribly fickle and unpredictable. So, the question arises: How can we mortals ever hope to follow Christ's great example of stalwart faithfulness, especially in the face of prolonged difficulty? Well, I believe that it can be done when we rid ourselves of the distractions that prevent us from following Jesus' lead. I'm talking about getting tough with those yearnings to always have our own way and the need to walk to the beat of our own drummer while belting out the song, "I Did It My Way." There's nothing wrong with expressing our individuality, but we shouldn't forget to seek and follow God while we're searching for our uniqueness.

Most of us don't want to admit it, but in the deepest recesses of our souls, we believe that the path to a more meaningful life is found in doing things our own way. Yet the Bible says, "Self-help is no help at all. Self-sacrifice is the way, my way, to saving yourself, your true self. What good would it do to get everything you want and lose you, the real you?" (Mark 8:35-36).

In other words, we need to totally surrender our need to dictate to God the path for our life. Just as Jesus laid down His life for us, He invites us to surrender our lives to Him. Yes, I know that it is not an equal exchange, because, let's face it, He died to do for us what we could never do for ourselves. But by sacrificing our desires for His, we allow the character of Christ to be revealed in us and for His presence to take up a comfortable residence in our hearts.

Yes, I said the dreaded S word, "sacrifice." In some circles, this word gets a bad rap. But to sacrifice simply means to surrender. So staying in step with God happens when we totally surrender our agenda for the joy of allowing Christ to take the lead in our life. We've got to give up something precious before we can get something precious in return.

LET'S GET IT STARTED

The good news is that every spiritual journey has a starting point. The bad news is that most people put off ever getting started. Procrastination is a negative side effect of the process of waiting for God. It occurs when we don't recognize the need to keep our spiritual lives active and fulfilling.

A worthy goal during this season is to avoid becoming a spiritual procrastinator. Someone once said that tomorrow is often the busiest day of the week. However, waiting for God is not synonymous with putting *everything* off until tomorrow. There are things that only God can do for us, and there are things that we must do for ourselves.

The tendency to procrastinate is so powerful during a divine delay that only those people with a fighting mentality win the battle. Let me illustrate the paralyzing power of procrastination. Imagine standing in the center of a boxing ring. The bell sounds, the crowd goes wild, and the match begins. Coming at you from each of the four corners is a different reason to put off maintaining intimacy with God. First, spiritual fatigue charges at you from the far left and lands a punch to the stomach. Next, the fear of tomorrow strikes a blow to your right temple, paralyzing your faith. Third, frustration sneaks up from behind, pulling you back into the past. Finally, a lack of focus, the most sinister member of the pack, throws a right hook to your eye to blind your spiritual vision.

Do you get the picture? These four foes—fatigue, fear of tomorrow, frustration and lack of focus—are the main reasons we put off moving ahead spiritually during a delay. Yet I have discovered that one of the best ways to win the battle over procrastination is through a strong commitment to the spiritual discipline of fasting coupled with prayer.

FASTING AND PRAYER

A regular diet of fasting and prayer will help us maintain our spiritual momentum by moving our affections toward God at a consistent pace. Oddly, I learned these secrets of fasting and prayer from a wise old woman in the Bible named Anna who knew how to wait for God. Luke writes, "Anna the prophetess was also there. . . . She was by now a very old woman. She had been married seven years and a widow for eighty-four. She never left the Temple area, worshiping night and day with her fastings and prayers" (Luke 2:36-37).

There is no way for us to know how many of those 84 years Anna spent in fasting, praying and waiting. What we do know is that she didn't stumble in her relationship with God during the process. We also know that she was rewarded for her sacrifice.

The story continues that Mary and Joseph went to the Temple to present baby Jesus to the priest. It was customary for young Jewish children to receive prayer and a blessing from their spiritual leaders. Luke tells us that, "At the very time Simeon was praying, [Anna] showed up, broke into an anthem of praise to God, and talked about the child to all who were waiting expectantly for the freeing of Jerusalem" (Luke 2:38). God pays great dividends when we surrender ourselves completely to Him.

It could be said that the opposite of procrastination is being proactive. This is what Anna did. The elderly Anna had so much discipline that she was able to wait for God in one place for a long, long time. Contrary to popular opinion, we should grow stronger and deeper while our destiny is being delayed. Like Anna, we must allow the years of hoping and praying to feed our passion for God.

How many times have you argued with the Lord about your present assignment, saying, "Lord, don't You know that I'm too old for this? I'm too tired; my mind is slow. I can't even afford to pay attention." I want to be like Anna, and I know that you do, too. I believe that she had a strong motivation—she was determined to see the promise of God revealed in her lifetime. Clearly, she was a woman of great spiritual discipline. She could have used any number of excuses to put off staying fresh for God, but she didn't. What was different about her?

Well, it must have been Anna's commitment to fasting that fueled her ability to stay constantly fresh and in step with God. Choosing to go on with God forces us to stop procrastinating and start living a more disciplined life. Both Jesus and Paul fasted and prayed before going on to new levels in God. When Jesus fasted for 40 days in the wilderness, He emerged with the focus, fire and conviction He needed to begin His mission. When Paul fasted for three days, his spiritual eyes were opened, enabling him to begin his spiritual journey.

WE SHOULD GROW STRONGER AND DEEPER WHILE OUR DESTINY IS BEING DELAYED. WE MUST ALLOW THE YEARS OF HOPING AND PRAYING TO FEED OUR PASSION FOR GOD.

To "fast" means to abstain from food for a specified period of time for spiritual reasons. It is simply an outward indication of an inward sincerity. Fasting lifts our focus from the natural to the spiritual because we deny our natural desire for food and spend increased time in God's Word and in prayer. The time we normally spend eating is now used for praying and pruning the heart of unwanted worries and cares. (For a quick guide to fasting, see the appendix at the end of this book.)

RUNNING FROM GOD

For much of my Christian experience (especially during times of divine delays), I have lived on a diet of fasting and prayer, and it has always resulted in a renewed hunger and thirst for God. But some years ago, I found that I needed to make a fresh commitment to this spiritual discipline.

For the first 10 years of our church's existence, I was the only pianist, worship leader and creative arts director in the church. Back then, I fasted on a regular basis, but God was calling me to do more. The arrival of another musician had been delayed, and I was feeling stretched beyond my capacity. The pace of daily ministry, coupled with my responsibilities as a wife and mother, had taken its toll on me. Wearing those three hats had left me spiritually empty and physically exhausted. I had lost my drive to grow in the things of God, and my spiritual motivation was gone.

When the time finally came to hire another musician, I was excited. I planned to step back from leading the music department. However, I soon awakened to the fact that my desires were not God's desires. Through a few close friends, God encouraged me to move to the next level of spiritual leadership. This required even more management of the music ministry, but less hands-on involvement. However, I was tired, and I merely wanted to put off the promotion.

I did my best to avoid doing the will of God. It was foolish to think that I could just close my ears to the Lord. He knew how to get my attention, and He did so in a very dramatic way. It was the spring of 1996, and I was on my way to a funeral for a friend who had just died of cancer. The highway was lined with beautiful green foliage on that sunny day. Suddenly, a huge oak tree fell directly in the path of my car. Strangely, as I looked around, I heard no wind, felt no rain, and could see no natural cause for the tree to fall in front of me. Miraculously, I drove right under the tree trunk just before it pounded down to the asphalt.

At that moment, I took a hard look at my life and realized that I had been given two things: a chance to live and a choice to make. I could either stay in step with God, or I could give up more than I'd bargained for. You guessed it—I chose to stop focusing on my fears so that I could better respond to God's leadership in my life.

In the days following this near-death experience, I reflected on how to stop procrastinating and press forward. I thought about the things I'd done in the past to stay in step with God and remembered the power of fasting coupled with prayer. Almost immediately, I began fasting for spiritual renewal to take place in my heart. Since then, I have never wrestled with that kind of fear, spiritual fatigue, lack of focus and frustration again. The power of those negative forces was broken, and I was free.

In the end, my challenge helped me to let go of the habit of putting off following and staying close to God. I had no other choice—I had to embrace change or face spiritual decay. I also had to make some key changes (this is just a nice way to say that I needed boundaries). Carving out more time in my life for rest and other things brought balance and healing.

FASTING FUELS A DISCIPLINED SPIRITUAL LIFE

I believe there are four important ways that fasting fuels a disciplined spiritual life and breaks the bondage of spiritual procrastination. Remember that fasting is an outward display of an inward desperation for God. The prophet Isaiah wrote, "Is not this the kind of fasting I have chosen: to loose the chains of injustice and untie the cords of the yoke, to set the oppressed free and break every yoke?" (Isa. 58:6, *NIV*).

1. Fasting Cures Spiritual Fatigue

Fasting renews our life spirit by allowing us to spend time renewing our relationship with the Lord. In his book *Fasting Can Change Your Life*, Pastor Leroy Lebeck tells how he achieved a new spiritual level of energy through this discipline:

> One of the things I enjoy most about fasting is that I really rest during the fast. I renew my strength and renew my spirit. I don't go to work: that means that I don't go to the church. I stay at home and finally get rest. I don't eat and get tired when I fast. I yield to that and go to sleep. When I get up, I read my Bible and read Christian books. When I get weary again, I let myself go to sleep. I have a hot tub out in the backyard. I sit in the Jacuzzi and read, pray, relax outside in a chair and enjoy the sunshine. The days I spend fasting there [are] a tremendous recouping of my strength and physical energy . . . Every time I fast I renew my spiritual energy level . . . I feel blessed."[1]

2. Fasting Empowers Us to Overcome the Fear of Failure

Not eating is a natural response when we're afraid. Most people can't even think about food if there is a threat of divorce, losing a job, financial collapse or a stressful ministry challenge. It is in times like these that we must seize the moment and fast for God's divine guidance and protection. In 2 Chronicles 20, the king of Judah came under attack by a great multitude of Moabites and Amonites. The Bible tells us that "[King] Jehoshaphat feared . . . and proclaimed a fast throughout all Judah" (v. 3, *NKJV*). In combination with fasting, Jehosha-phat led the people in a prayer of helplessness. In desperation, they cried out to the Lord, saying, "For we have no power . . . nor do we know what to do, but our eyes are on You" (v. 12, *NKJV*). The story ends with the Moabites and Amonites attacking and killing each other instead of the people of Judah.

3. Fasting Helps Overcome Feelings of Frustration

When we are frustrated, we usually see our responsibilities as burdens, which makes it more difficult for us to accomplish tasks in a timely manner. We may also be frustrated because we have placed unrealistic expectations on ourselves and on others. When we approach a task, we should focus on what we can *realistically* accomplish, rather than on what we can *ideally* accomplish, and do our best in the time allowed. The time we invest should be in direct proportion to the magnitude of our desire. By changing our perspective, we'll make an outlet for frustration to bleed out of our system.

4. Fasting Helps Restore Lost Focus

Once we overcome the initial pangs of hunger, fasting often leads us to a state of lightness and clarity. When we are not obsessed with getting food, our thoughts and feelings have an opportunity to settle into deeper and loftier places. This loftier place is really the restoration of lost focus.

PRAYING FOR RENEWED PASSION

Our spiritual passion is like a fire that must be stoked. When we spend time adding the wood of prayer to the flame, the wind of the Spirit comes to fan the fire, and it becomes so hot that even a rainstorm of disappointment can't douse it. On the other hand, if we don't feed the fire of our spiritual passion, it will flicker out and die. When John Wesley was asked why so many people came to hear him preach, he said, "I just set myself on fire and the people come to watch me burn!"

Now here's the question: Are you so passionate about God that you'll cooperate with His timing for your life *today*? Is your passion for Him so strong that you are committed to pleasing Him, no matter how long He causes you to wait? The promise you await may not come today, but I encourage you to wait expectantly and patiently. Set yourself on fire by making a commitment to remain spiritually fresh. This is God's desire for you. In Galatians 4:18, Paul makes clear the need for us to continually pursue passion in our spiritual lives when he says, "But it is good to be zealously affected always in a good thing, and not only when I am present with you" (*KJV*).

So what do we do when God gives us an assignment and we can't seem to muster up any passion for the mission? We turn to prayer. Prayer is the vehicle whereby we can get the help, comfort and guidance we so desperately need. I like to cut through all the fancy definitions and simply define prayer as *talking to God*. I believe that our God is a speaking God, and that if we talk to Him, He'll respond. He'll give us a renewed passion for cooperating with His timing.

Prayer is to our spiritual life what gasoline is to a car engine. Separately, the two are dynamic, but together they are powerfully effective at moving us deeper in God's love—regardless of the circumstances. Prayer helps us rise above the lethargy and lackadaisical haze that at times overwhelms us during a divine delay.

I believe that Anna knew this secret and practiced a special kind of prayer to ward off procrastination. The Bible calls it "unceasing prayer," which is expressed in repeated, heartfelt petitions to God. It is this sincere repetition of specific prayers that increases the spiritual vitality and temperament of our heart. Unceasing prayer creates a fluid, free-flowing conversation with God that transforms our very nature. This fluidity is exactly the kind of spiritual water needed to get us moving and flowing toward God.

The great philosopher Jean-Pierre De Caussade wrote about what happens to someone whose life is full of perpetual prayer: "The soul, light as a feather, fluid as water, innocent as a child responds to every movement of grace like a floating balloon."[2] Notice that this kind of prayer doesn't create *communication* with God, but *conversation* with God. There is a huge difference between communication and conversation. Communication implies a transfer of information from one person to another. But conversation, although information is still being exchanged, is much more personal and intimate. It is a dialogue consisting of a two-way exchange of thoughts, ideas and information.

Many years ago, I learned that an often-repeated practice eventually becomes an addiction and that an addiction eventually becomes a passion. So it is with establishing the habit of unceasing prayer. Psychologist William James declared, "The man who has daily inured [trained] himself to habits of *concentrated attention*, *energetic volition*, and *self denial* will stand like a tower when everything rocks about him and when his softer fellow mortals are winnowed like chaff in the blast."[3] This is a great description of the power of unceasing prayer.

MAKING UNCEASING PRAYER A DAILY DISCIPLINE

I want to offer you a practical plan for making unceasing prayer a daily discipline so that you can live passionately for God regardless of what season you're in. It's a two-step program that really works. To start, make it a priority to pray for three things. Then earnestly and repeatedly ask God to birth in you the three habits that Dr. James mentioned above:

1. Concentrated attention or an ability to maintain an unbroken focus on God. Eliminating a broken focus from your life won't happen automatically. Having a broken focus is like a stubborn household pest that multiplies and becomes a bigger problem if left unchecked. Each day, you must choose the things that occupy your thoughts.

2. Energetic volition, or an enthusiastic and willing heart to do the will of God.

3. Self-denial, or the ability to avoid doing the things that rob you of a passionate life.

Next, begin to view mundane activities as opportunities for unceasing, silent prayer. I call this practice taking a *prayer break,* although it does not require you to stop whatever you're doing to find a place of solitude or privacy. You can take a prayer break while washing the dishes, driving the car, waiting in line at the grocery store or riding in an elevator. These activities all qualify as opportunities for a prayer break and will increase your ability to concentrate on growing in intimacy with God.

When I first started practicing the prayer break principle, I was skeptical about it. I had visions of getting so lost in my thoughts toward God that I'd end up walking around in a stupor. I saw myself missing my exit on the freeway or being so distracted by the people and sounds around me that maintaining a real conversation with God would be almost impossible.

But none of this ever happened. The human mind has the ability to focus on more than one thing at a time. Think about it—all day long we think about one, two or three different things while we're doing something else. When I practice unceasing prayer in this manner, my mind is more productive because I am not distracted by insignificant issues. Taking prayer breaks throughout the day has caused me to become more intentional about harnessing my thought life. Over time, I have become increasingly more engaged with God's presence as I have focused on conversing with Him moment by moment.

PRAY LIKE DAVID PRAYED

God wants our heart to belong exclusively to Him. His greatest hope is for us to daily feast on His love and walk in His ways. Psalm 86:11 says, "Teach me Your way, O Lord; I will walk in Your truth; Unite my heart to fear Your name" (NKJV). In other words, David, recognizing his lack of focus, was saying to the Lord, "Do not let my heart have many allegiances or affections."

Often, when promises have been delayed, distractions, allegiances and new affections try to move in. Our struggle with the cares and concerns of this life will certainly cry out for our attention. For many, the struggle can become mentally and emotionally overwhelming. Consider the man in his fifties whose mind is filled with thoughts of his unfulfilled goals, or the lonely wife who is distracted by the call of her unmet emotional needs, or the young professional who is preoccupied with the call to succeed.

We all struggle to maintain an undivided heart. However, we must realize that there is a purpose behind it all. If we're patient,

the fruit of struggle will prove to be our testimony, as the following story shows:

> One day a man found the cocoon of a butterfly. Soon
> a small opening appeared on the surface. He sat and
> watched for the butterfly for several hours as it strug-
> gled to force its body through that little hole. Then it
> seemed to stop making any progress. It appeared as if
> it had gotten as far as it could and it could go no fur-
> ther.
>
> So the man decided to help the butterfly. He took
> a pair of scissors and snipped off the remaining bit of
> the cocoon. The butterfly then emerged easily. But it
> had a swollen body and small, shriveled wings.
>
> The man continued to watch the butterfly because
> he expected that, at any moment, the wings would
> enlarge and expand to be able to support the body,
> which would contract in time. Neither happened! In
> fact, the butterfly spent the rest of its life crawling
> around with a swollen body and shriveled wings. It never
> was able to fly.
>
> What the man in his kindness and haste did not
> understand was that the restricting cocoon and the
> struggle required for the butterfly to get through the
> tiny opening were God's way of forcing fluid from
> the body of the butterfly into its wings so that it
> would be ready for flight once it achieved its freedom
> from the cocoon.
>
> Sometimes struggles are exactly what we need in
> our life. If God allowed us to go through our life with-
> out any obstacles, it would cripple us. We would not be
> as strong as what we could have been. And we could
> never fly.[4]

God has given us the ability to turn the struggles of this life into a passion for spiritual progress. The Bible puts it this way: "These hard times are small potatoes compared to the coming good times, the lavish celebration prepared for us" (2 Cor. 4:17). Even the butterfly possessed a passion for the future. Otherwise, it would not have pursued its freedom from the cocoon. The same kind of passion needed for the butterfly is the passion that God wants us to have for staying in step with Him.

This is what the Christian life is about. Paul stated, "I've got my eye on the goal, where God is beckoning us onward—to Jesus" (Phil. 3:13). With spiritual progress comes freedom. Yet this freedom does not focus on the things of the past. Its focus is the freedom we have to pursue God with all of our heart, soul, mind and strength. This kind of passion releases us to stick with the delay while avoiding inertia.

Right now, you may not look or feel like a fully developed, beautiful butterfly. To some, you may even appear to be an ugly caterpillar. But soon, you'll have wings to fly. It doesn't matter what the situation around you looks like. You are being perfected for your purpose and are being designed for your destiny. Right now, you may be considering a plan to take a detour around the struggle, but a shortcut will only lead to weakness instead of strength. You must learn to stick with the struggle.

Early one morning during my own quest for an undivided heart, this cry arose from somewhere deep inside of me:

YOU MAY BE CONSIDERING A PLAN TO TAKE A DETOUR AROUND THE STRUGGLE, BUT A SHORTCUT WILL ONLY LEAD TO WEAKNESS. YOU MUST LEARN TO STICK WITH THE STRUGGLE.

Lord, with Your help I will not allow my attention and my allegiance to be entertained by anything or anyone else but You. I will only permit my heart to be enthralled by Your beauty, engaged by Your majesty, entangled in Your grace, and enraptured by Your laughter. I live to be engrossed in Your wisdom, enmeshed in Your will and enchanted by Your love. Every moment of every day I am captivated, fascinated, spellbound, awestruck and mesmerized by You. Let no man, woman, worry or care take center stage in my heart, play on the big screen of my mind, or stand in the spotlight of my gaze. I belong exclusively to You.

There are secrets to creating a passion for progress while we wait for God. These steps are based on the principle that if we prepare our heart through fasting and prayer, an enthusiasm for God will come. In short, preparation always fuels passion.

DON'T GET STUCK

So often we get stuck on one step of the spiritual ladder—unable to get past a disappointment or a struggle in life. I know people who have stopped growing spiritually simply because God did not answer a particular prayer in their life. Because their prayer was not answered, they no longer pray the way they used to or read and study the Bible the way they used to. Their passion for a deeper relationship with God flickered, fizzled out and died. Many have even boycotted the Body of Christ by withdrawing from church and other believers. Their hearts have grown cold toward God.

What a waste of potential. These people have robbed themselves of a lot of pleasure on this side of heaven. We must refuse to be a causality of circumstance. When God says no, we need to take it like a champ—like one who trusts in God's wisdom. We need to make a vow to never stop staying in step with Him.

We need to stick with God through the delay, but not get spiritually stuck. We need to stop waiting for tomorrow before deciding to stay in step with God.

> So stop waiting until you finish school,
> until you go back to school,
> until you lose 10 pounds,
> until you gain 10 pounds,
> until you have kids,
> until your kids leave the house,
> until you get married,
> until your marriage is healed,
> until you get a new car or home,
> until your car or home is paid off,
> until spring, until summer,
> until fall, until winter,
> to decide that there is no better time
> than right now to be happy . . .
> Happiness is a journey, not a destination.

This life is only temporary. We are not physical beings on a temporary spiritual assignment. We are spiritual beings on a temporary physical assignment. We must make our quest for a consistent spiritual journey unconditional. The only prerequisite is staying in step with God. There's no need to wait. Loving and serving Him are always in season—there are no time limits on this task.

SURVIVAL SECRETS
Remember

The Picture from the Past: You never need to miss a beat with God. In the Bible, Anna had so much discipline that she was able to stay in one place long enough to see the promise.

The Practice for the Present: Engage in unceasing prayer and regular fasting to defeat spiritual fatigue, fear, frustration and a lack of focus.

The Promise for the Future: You don't have to see the end from the beginning—just follow your leader. "Anyone who intends to come with me has to let me lead. You're not in the driver's seat; I am. Don't run. . . . Follow me and I'll show you how" (Mark 8:34).

Notes

1. Jerry Falwell and Elmer Towns, eds., *Fasting Can Change Your Life* (Ventura, CA: Regal Books, 1998).
2. Jean-Pierre De Caussade, *The Sacrament of the Present Moment* (San Francisco: HarperSanFrancisco, 1989).
3. Dick Eastman, *No Easy Road* (Grand Rapids, MI: Chosen Books, 2003).
4. "The Butterfly," After-hours Inspirational Stories. http://www.inspiration alstories.com/10/1006.html.

CHAPTER SEVEN

Confirming Your Purpose in a Prison

*USE ALL YOUR SKILL TO PUT ME TOGETHER;
I WAIT TO SEE YOUR FINISHED PRODUCT.*
PSALM 25:21

Vanessa is a vibrant and powerfully gifted singer and songwriter. She has been involved in our church for more than a decade. Over the years, life has deposited some deep scars on her heart. In a short period of time, she suffered a number of heartbreaking tragedies. These events caused her to feel like a hostage of time and circumstance.

Living in a divine delay can make us feel as if we're trapped in a prison. This sense of being bound and chained to the present dilemma can be discouraging—especially when we're facing multiple disappointments. Yet, hope springs to life when we understand that God can confirm our purpose even while we're seemingly enduring a prison-like situation.

One blustery winter day, while making her way across an icy parking lot, Vanessa fell and severely damaged her ankle. Shortly thereafter, she received the sad news that her mother had succumbed to colon cancer. In the midst of all of this, Vanessa suffered two devastating miscarriages, with the second pregnancy ending in a stillbirth. The baby's funeral was particularly heart-wrenching, because she and her husband, Ray, had had a difficult time in conceiving a child. Finally, Vanessa and Ray endured several seasons of financial lack due to the tight job market in New Jersey. During this journey, I was able to speak words of comfort to Vanessa and hold her hand as she wiped away many tears.

We're in the midst of a prison-like season when our ability to move forward is restricted by unmovable barriers or unalterable circumstances. Prisons are uncomfortable places in which to live, but God miraculously uses them for our benefit. How does He do this? God has the power to supernaturally and sovereignly make our gifts, abilities and talents shine and become noticeable to the people around us—even when we're in a prison-like situation. It's as if He somehow makes us a light in the midst of darkness. Suddenly, people in places of influence, power or authority begin to recognize our work and appreciate our worth. God then uses their influence and connections as bridges to our destiny. So it was with Vanessa.

As a young girl, Vanessa had dreamed of entering the world of high-fashion design. She had flare and an edgy style, and she excelled in her studies at a fashion college in New York City. But Vanessa was surprised when one of her professors began to encourage her to draw illustrations for children's books. Vanessa felt that illustrating wasn't as artistically rewarding or profitable as fashion design, so she set her sights in other directions. However, she was quite discouraged by the professor's remarks concerning her initial career goals, and she began to feel as if her dreams of becoming a designer were arrested and sent to prison.

While praying one day, Vanessa felt impressed to revisit the idea of illustrating children's books. She wrote a few lines and drew some pictures to go along with them. Soon, it became a private passion. Vanessa created silly stories and rhymes with reason, as well as rhymes with no reason. Deep inside her heart, she hoped that something significant would come of her artwork.

Over time, Vanessa's patience with her work turned into frustration, and then into a sense of failure. However, one day as she was about to throw away some of her drawings, an unexpected visitor dropped in. At the time, Vanessa didn't know it, but the stranger was an editor for a children's book publisher.

The editor looked at the drawings and was astonished by their beauty and creativity. That afternoon, the editor told Vanessa that if she would create some stories to go along with the illustrations, the editor would see if her company might publish them. Today, Vanessa is a published illustrator of children's stories and an author to boot. The events of that afternoon were a sovereign set-up—God at work confirming Vanessa's purpose in her prison.

CHOOSE TO ACCEPT THE SOVEREIGNTY OF GOD

Making the most of a prison-like season is easier when we acknowledge that God is in control of our destiny. When we acknowledge the sovereignty of God, we recognize that He is the one in charge and that we are neither independent nor autonomous. This means giving up the right to decide our path in life by adopting the perspective that we are not our own—we have been bought with a price (see 1 Cor. 6:19-20).

So we are, in essence, a prisoner—a prisoner for Christ. The apostle Paul writes, "As a prisoner for the Lord, then, I urge you to live a life worthy of the calling you have received" (Eph. 4:1, *NIV*). Having this view of our spiritual position means that at times our prayers should be, "Lord, help me to accept Your sovereign will," not "Lord, please change this situation."

God's sovereignty can be frightening. The great Scottish preacher Horatius Bonar put it this way: "If [God] gets His will, I am afraid that I shall not get mine. It comes out, moreover, that the God about whose love I was so fond of speaking, is a God to whom I cannot trust myself implicitly for eternity."[1] However, if we're going to make it through to the end of our prison-like season, we'll have to trust God while we're in this time of waiting. One of the secrets to experiencing the favor of God is to yield to the sovereignty of God. Our blessings are tied to our obedience.

A Sovereign Setup

God's sovereignty reminds us that it's really all about Him, not about us. This was never truer than in the life of Joseph. In the Bible, we find the powerful account of this young man who had been given a dream by God. In reality, it was God's dream for Joseph, and it carried a greater purpose and scope than he could have ever imagined. Isn't this how our Father usually works? We only know and understand a small part of His plans for us. Our God-given dream is likely destined to help not just us but also those in our home, on our jobs, and in our communities.

In the dream, Joseph, who was the second-to-last child in his family, ruled over his father, mother and older brothers (see Gen. 37:6-9). When Joseph shared his dream, his father thought the dream made no sense at all. When his brothers heard about it, they became so bitter and jealous that they sold him into slavery (see vv. 12-28). Joseph's brothers then covered up their wickedness by telling their father that Joseph had been killed by wild animals. Through a series of events, Joseph ended up as a slave in Egypt, where he was falsely accused of rape and thrown into prison (see Gen. 39).

There are times in all of our lives when we will face situations that seem unfair or unjust. These times cause us to question God's heart toward us. Horatius Bonar once said, "Man's dislike at God's sovereignty arises from his suspicion of God's heart."[2] Yet it's important that we remember two simple things: (1) God's sovereignty is good for us, and (2) God's sovereignty shows His loves for us. We must trust that the Lord is still in control of our lives and that He uses prison-like seasons for our good, for the good of others, and to confirm our purpose.

Making the Best of a Bad Situation

Joseph chose to make the best of a bad situation. In the dungeon of life, he became known as a leader and interpreter of dreams. The prison officials entrusted him with more and more responsibility, and his fellow prisoners trusted him with their dreams. How was this young man able to exhibit such courage and character? What was the driving force behind his staying power while locked up in prison?

I believe that Joseph somehow knew that he was in the middle of a sovereign setup. He must have realized that, even while he was in that tight spot, opportunity for personal progress continued to present itself. So, day after day and year after year, he put his best foot forward and put his heart on autopilot. Sometimes, we must automatically do the right thing when we don't know what else to do.

Joseph's prison was simply a prelude to meeting with the most powerful man in the world. After Joseph had spent two years in the dungeon, the Pharaoh had two troubling dreams about an impending famine. He sent for all the magicians and sages, but no one could interpret his dreams. Then the head cup-bearer spoke up and said:

> I just now remembered something—I'm sorry, I should have told you this long ago. Once when Pharaoh got angry with his servants, he locked me and the head baker in the house of the captain of the guard. We both had dreams on the same night, each dream with its own meaning. It so happened that there was a young Hebrew slave there with us . . . and he interpreted them for us,

each dream separately. Things turned out just as he interpreted (Gen. 41:9-13).

Look at how God works His sovereignty in our lives: Even when a relationship is not ideal (the way that Joseph helped two people from very different backgrounds and beliefs in an Egyptian dungeon), God brings something good out of it. Isn't God's sovereignty amazing? We may be surprised to learn how intricately our lives are connected to others—even our enemies or partners in prison. We need to remain faithful to God and keep our gifts and talents active, because "when a man's ways are pleasing to the Lord, he makes even his enemies live at peace with him" (Prov. 16:7, *NIV*).

It is up to us to make sure that our actions toward others are pleasing to the Lord. God is willing and able to change the hearts of our enemies, but we need to give Him something to work with. We should expect Him to give us sovereign favor in the sight of our teachers, employers, neighbors and others we meet. But we should not assume that this favor is automatic. Rather, we are required to ask God to act on our behalf.

God Confirms Joseph's Purpose

Pharaoh listened to the cupbearer's report and sent for Joseph at once. Joseph was immediately brought from his jail cell. After he had shaved and changed his clothes, he was brought before Pharaoh. "I've heard that just by hearing a dream you can interpret it," Pharaoh said (Gen. 41:15). Joseph answered, "Not I, but God. God will set Pharaoh's mind at ease" (v. 16).

Joseph listened carefully, interpreted the dreams, and then told Pharaoh what he needed to do. The advice that Joseph gave to Pharaoh showed amazing resourcefulness and confirmed Joseph's purpose as a man of leadership. It also showed that he knew how to be productive in hard times. Joseph then said,

"Pharaoh needs to look for a wise and experienced man and put him in charge of the country. This way the country won't be devastated by the famine" (vv. 33,36).

Pharaoh said to his officials, "Isn't this the man we need? Are we going to find anyone else who has God's spirit in him like this?" (v. 38). Pharaoh removed his signet ring from his finger and slipped it on Joseph's hand. He outfitted him in robes of the best linen and put a gold chain around his neck. He put a chariot at Joseph's disposal, and as Joseph rode through the streets, people shouted, "Bravo!" (see vv. 41-43). Pharaoh told Joseph, "I am Pharaoh, but no one in Egypt will make a single move without your stamp of approval" (v. 44). Do you see the power of accepting the sovereignty of God even while you're awaiting His promises? The next time you're tempted to give up or to stop being your best, just remember Joseph's jailhouse experience.

Most of us wonder why bad things happen to good people. Why does God allow a wrench to be thrown into the spokes of our wheels and bring life to a screeching halt? Most often, we feel that we are the authors of our own demise. Joseph probably blamed himself for his troubles. After all, didn't his brothers sell him into slavery after he told them about his dreams of one day ruling over his family? He probably thought, *I should have kept my big mouth shut.*

In the problem you are facing, you have probably asked similar questions. While there are no easy answers, the bottom line is that God's sovereignty works for us even when our mistakes

WHEN WE ARE IN A DIVINE DELAY AND FEEL LIKE A PRISONER, WE NEED TO ALWAYS REMEMBER THAT THE SOVEREIGNTY OF GOD IS AT WORK ALL AROUND US.

work against us. I think that God may factor our blunders into the overall scheme of things, and that He somehow intercepts these mistakes before they get in the way of His will.

Joseph's skill in interpreting dreams got him noticed by Pharaoh. God sovereignly used Joseph's prison and his persecutors to confirm Joseph's purpose in life. When we are in a divine delay and feel like a prisoner, we need to always remember that the sovereignty of God is at work all around us.

FINDING FAVOR WITH INFLUENTIAL PEOPLE

There's one other amazing thing about this story. God used Joseph to interpret the dreams of others *before* his own dreams came to pass, which proves the saying, "What you make happen for others, God will make happen for you." Proverbs 11:25 puts it this way: "The one who blesses others is abundantly blessed; those who help others are helped." If Joseph had allowed discouragement to hinder the use of his gifts and his abilities in the prison, he never would have been elevated to a higher place of service. His purpose may never have been confirmed.

When we come to the end of a divine delay, we'll know and understand more about the nature and character of God. One of the greatest gifts we receive may be our own acceptance of the fact that God is not only sovereign but also omnipotent. While His sovereignty may sting at times (because it is misunderstood), it will prove to be sweet in the end. It may even give way to a divine encounter. So it was with Joseph. He eventually comforted his brothers with the statement, "You intended to harm me, but God intended it for good to accomplish what is now being done, the saving of many lives" (Gen. 50:20, *NIV*). Joseph realized that God was involved with his being sold into slavery.

Joseph's painful ordeal with slavery and imprisonment became a platform for a demonstration of divine favor. Having

God's favor on our life simply means that we are pleasing to Him. In turn, God causes us to be pleasing and desirable to others. So, the kind of favor that Joseph experienced was not just the favor of God, but also multidimensional favor. He was pleasing and desirable to God *and* to others. Having favor with God and with others while waiting for the Lord to change our circumstances will set us up for a providential encounter.

Thankfully, the Bible teaches us that we can have the favor of the Lord by praying for it and then expecting it. Nehemiah did just that when he prayed, "O Lord, let your ear be attentive to the prayer of this your servant and to the prayer of your servants who delight in revering your name. Give your servant success today by granting him favor in the presence of this man [the king]" (Neh. 1:11, *NIV*).

I am amazed at how God gives me favor with all kinds of people. I have had the opportunity to work with and counsel many influential men and women as they went through a divine delay. Some were doctors, some were lawyers, some were business executives and ministry leaders, and some were in the arts. I've found most of these individuals to be people of great character, discipline and integrity. I've watched as they have lead others through stressful challenges while they, themselves, were feeling like prisoners of time. As they leaned on me to help them hold it together, I learned to do four important things.

1. Be a Covenant Keeper

"Never let loyalty and kindness get away from you! Wear them like a necklace; write them deep within your heart. Then you will find favor with both God and people, and you will gain a good reputation" (Prov. 3:3-4, *NLT*). A covenant is an agreement or contract between two parties or individuals. Men and women of influence don't usually make light of any kind of contract. So, if someone comes to you for help, or if you happen to be the one assisting others with a problem, realize that you may be entering into a kind of unspoken relational or professional pact with them.

They will expect you to be a person of the utmost honesty, confidentiality and integrity. You must never take the relationship for granted. Remember that regardless of their profile, their lives are filled with stress. At times, you will probably view the underside of their bellies and see them at their worst. However, always guard against becoming slack in your respect and commitment to them.

2. Focus on What's Important Rather than What's Immediate
Even successful people need help keeping the right focus during difficult times. You can serve as a moral and emotional anchor for them when the storms of life are raging. In the book of Romans, the apostle Paul states that there are three things worth focusing on in this life: "The important things are living right with God, peace, and joy in the Holy Spirit. Anyone who serves Christ by living this way is pleasing God and will be accepted by other people" (Rom. 14:17-18, NCV). In other words, help your friends in high places to focus on righteousness, peace and joy in the Holy Spirit.

How? First, aid them in doing the right thing. Realize that your own right living is probably what attracted these people to you. Teach them to follow Christ despite the ethical, moral or spiritual challenges before them. Also, help them to understand God's peace by modeling it. A person of influence has enough stress without having frantic and stressed-out people around them. Your attitude can have a calming influence on their mental and emotional state.

Teach and impart the joy of the Holy Spirit. You can do this by modeling a quiet confidence in God. This is actually the definition of the word "joy" in the New Testament. Joy is not a giddy kind of emotion. It is a calm assurance in God, especially in His ability to resolve your problems. Remember how Joseph directed Pharaoh to trust in God? He said, "Not I, but God. God will set Pharaoh's mind at ease" (Gen. 41:16).

3. Don't Try to Flatter Influential People

Daniel 1:9 says, "Now God had caused the official to show favor and sympathy to Daniel" (*NIV*). Praying for favor with other people is more effective than manipulating your way into their good graces. Allow God to bring attention to your good works.

4. Realize Your Power Comes from God

Remember that there are only two kinds of power in the world. There is power that comes from God, and then there is every other kind of power—worldly power. Worldly power has never been (and will never be) any match for the power of God. We run into problems when we forget this truth. Psalm 89:17 says, "Our power is based on your favor" (*NLT*). And Psalm 5:12 states, "Surely, O Lord, you bless the righteous; you surround them with your favor as with a shield" (*NIV*). We are God's children, His chosen, His elect.

People who are really committed to God will sometimes be criticized and persecuted. But if we're making a difference for God, we can't expect Satan to just sit back and do nothing to hinder us. The Bible teaches that even when we're under attack from the enemy, we can still pray for God's favor.

BECOME PRODUCTIVE IN YOUR PRISON

Vanessa and Joseph overcame the atrophy that is so common to those who wait for God. They both remained productive in their prison situation, and so can you. All too often we think, *As soon as I get out of this situation, that's when I'll do something. As soon as I get over this sickness, that's when I'll get focused.* But God wants us to use our talents, resources and abilities right where we are—not just when we get out of the prison-like situation. This involves doing the right thing, even when the wrong thing is happening to us. God wants us to be a blessing to others, even when no one is being a blessing to us. If we do the right thing even though the wrong things seem to be happening to us, we are sowing the seeds for God to bring us up to a higher level.

Some time ago, I heard about a young man who was diagnosed with a terminal lung disease. He waited for a lung transplant for a number of years, but no donor could be found. His condition was so severe that he couldn't even breathe on his own. He was forced to carry an oxygen tank everywhere he went. He was constantly in and out of the hospital due to his susceptibility to respiratory infections. It seemed as if he had a good reason to resign from life and just give up.

Yet despite his sickness, this young man was positive and productive. Would you believe that he never requested a handicap sticker for his car? He didn't want that kind of image in front of him. He never went around feeling sorry for himself, saying, "God, why me? When are things going to change?"

Amazingly, this young man even went out and landed a job. He excelled at that position and received promotion after promotion. He remained involved in his church and stayed active in its youth ministry. He was a giver and a worker, the kind of person who left each place he went better than it was before he arrived. In the midst of his prison, he continued to live a productive life.

One day, he received a call from the doctor. "There's good news!" the doctor said. "We've finally found a donor." A few days later, he had a successful transplant. Today, he doesn't need the oxygen tank. He can take in a deep breath of fresh air completely on his own. He's now living a normal, healthy life. Yet he could have easily had a negative attitude and thought, *As soon as I get free from this disease, I'll start helping other people. As soon as God heals me, I'll start using my gifts and talents. Right now it's just too difficult. I have too many limitations.* This young man had the mentality of a victor, not of a prisoner.

No matter what we face in life, we need to make up our minds that it's not going to stop us from being our very best. We can't allow life's circumstances to stop us from attending church, from working hard, or from welcoming joy into our life. We have to be determined to dig our heels in and say, "It doesn't matter what it looks like. I'm going to be positive and productive right here in my prison."

What can you learn from this? Always embrace the sovereignty of God, for resisting it only leads to an abortion of the very thing you're trying to conceive. Why not give in now? Your yielded heart may be the very thing that accelerates the day of your liberation. Ask God to help you accept His will for this season in your life.

BECOME BETTER AT BEING YOU

Human beings tend to be addicted to thinking about the past and how things *should* have been. Because we are creatures of habit, we also tend to continue behaving the way we did in the past. Yet the longer we focus on the past, the more deeply our bad habits become ingrained in us. As a result, it is harder to change our behavior and our view of the future.

People are always anxious to improve their circumstances but are often unwilling to improve themselves. Consequently, they remain bound. But Joseph was different. He became better and better at leading, even though he was unjustly imprisoned. He was obviously willing to improve himself despite his physical constraints and limited resources.

Think about it. Who taught Joseph what to do? I believe that Joseph probably honed his skills by watching and imitating the successful leaders that he witnessed at work. The Bible encourages us to learn by observing others. In Hebrews 6:12, we read, "We do not want you to become lazy, but to imitate those who through faith and patience inherit what has been promised" (*NIV*). What do you want to be? Find people who are doing it and then go out and study their practices. Train in the same way that they trained. Read what they read. Do what they did. The principles of greatness can be learned. Someone once said, "I pretended to be somebody I wanted to be until finally I became that person or he became me."

Also, believe that with God's help, you *can* change. It's not too late for you to soar, even though your mortality may be screaming such bad news as, "You're too old," "You're too slow," or "You don't have enough training." The good news is that you're not dead yet. If there are things in your life that you'd like to change, remember that you have something much more precious than money: You have time. At this stage of your life, there may be dreams you forgot about or never could have pursued until now. It's only too late if you stop now.

But you will never change your life until you change something you do each day. Your outcome will be affected by the choices you make on a daily basis. Act today and you'll reap a wonderful harvest tomorrow. The great inventor Charles F. Kettering once said, "You can't have a better tomorrow if you are thinking about yesterday all the time."

YOU WILL NEVER CHANGE YOUR LIFE UNTIL YOU CHANGE SOMETHING YOU DO EACH DAY. YOUR OUTCOME WILL BE AFFECTED BY THE CHOICES YOU MAKE ON A DAILY BASIS.

YOU'RE A MASTERPIECE WAITING TO BE REVEALED

Prisoners of time have trouble being objective about their lives. You probably don't realize that you may be one of God's masterpieces waiting to be revealed. David wrote, "Use all your skill to put me together; I wait to see your finished product" (Ps. 25:21).

But isn't it interesting how masterpieces are seldom made in one day? Similarly, they are seldom made in the open before critical eyes. Most great works of art are birthed over a long period of time while the artist works in solitary confinement. Isn't it also interesting how the process depends totally on the artist—on his skill and his pace? He alone determines when the finished product is revealed. God's masterpieces are never unveiled until He says, "It is time."

Some time ago, I learned about George Frederic Handel's unique prison-like season. Although he was a virtuoso organist, his occasional commercial success was all too often met with great financial disaster. He regularly bounced back from one failure after another. Over time, these setbacks took their toll on his body, until finally his health began to fail. By 1741, he was drowning in debt, and it seemed certain that he would be arrested and thrown into debtor's prison.

One day, Handel accepted a commission to compose a piece of music for a friend. As he set out to work on the music now known the world over as the *Messiah,* Handel became so absorbed in his work that he rarely left his room and barely stopped working long enough to eat. In a little less than a week, Part One of one of the greatest musical masterpieces in history was completed. In another nine days, Handel finished Part Two. And in six more days, Part Three was completed. Remarkably, Handel completed the orchestration in two days. In just 24 days—an unbelievably short period of time—the 260-page magnum opus was finished.

A friend who visited him during that time found the composer sobbing with intense emotion. Later, as Handel groped for words to describe his experience, he quoted the apostle Paul by saying, "Whether it was in the body or out of the body [when I wrote it] I do not know" (2 Cor. 12:2, *NIV*).

God was in it all the time. Handel's purpose in life was confirmed as he spent those 21 days in a sovereignly ordained prison. There were no bars or guards forcing him to stay, only a sense of God's divine timing.

THE PRISONS GOD CREATES

God ordains different kinds of prisons for different situations, and for people with different destinies. Some prisons are involuntary and sovereignly orchestrated, as in the case of Joseph. However, others require an act of humility and submission on our part. Sometimes, God awaits our willingness to submit to uncomfortable and difficult situations.

For example, God told the great and mighty prophet Elijah to go and wait by a brook for ravens to feed him carrion, the dead or decaying flesh of an animal. Elijah humbled himself and sat and ate by the brook until the brook dried up. God then told Elijah to travel almost 100 miles to a town called Zarephath. There, he would be fed by a widow. Imagine this powerful prophet having to approach a lowly widow for food. He humbled himself and did what he was told. Elijah found the widow looking for sticks to build a fire for her last meal, after which she was prepared to die of hunger. God responded to the prophet's obedience by multiplying the widow's meager food supply, and she did not go hungry.

In his book *Perfect Trust*, Charles Swindoll puts it this way:

God may be leading you somewhere such as Zarephath, somewhere that doesn't make much sense. I want to encourage you: don't try to make sense out of it, just go. If God leads you to stay in a difficult situation and you have peace that you are to stay, don't analyze it; stay. Do your part. Do what he tells you to do, for his promises often hinge on obedience. God told Elijah to get up and go, so he got up and went. God told the widow to fix the meal and she went and fixed it. They did their part and God did His part—they never ran out of food.

That doesn't mean that they had a banquet. They had simple, little bread cakes morning, noon and night. But they had food. Often, God's provisions are just enough. But don't fail to thank Him and trust Him. Maybe you don't have the job you wanted. Maybe you don't have the position you planned. But His provisions are just enough and just right for the time.

When God creates a prison experience for you, learn to go with the flow. Learn to draw closer to the Lord. Strive to become more passionate about the work of the Lord.

THE PRISON WILL PASS

It does not matter what kind of prison you're in. Trust me—it will pass. It will pass and you'll see how God worked while you worried. It will pass and you'll see in the mirror a man or woman with a deep and abiding confidence in God. You'll look in the mirror and wonder why you can't remember the pain and the shame of it all, because freedom will feel so good. I know because I've been there.

Your personal prison of shame, disappointment and feelings of rejection will not last forever. I know that the sense of being bound and chained to this present time can be crippling. But hope really does spring to life with the understanding that God can and does use your prison-like experiences to confirm your calling. After the prison doors are opened, after you've been unveiled as a magnificent Master's piece, then you'll be free to live life to the fullest. I am hopeful that by then, you'll be so comfortable with being a prisoner of the Lord that the invisible chains and the bars will have lost their power over you. Don't settle for a limited perspective of your prison-like season. There's more to life than what you can see between those unyielding prison bars.

SURVIVAL SECRETS
Remember

The Picture from the Past: Know that the sovereignty of God is at work all around you. It may sting now, but in the end it will be sweet.

The Practice for the Present: Become productive in your prison.

The Promise for the Future: Let God give you favor with people of influence. Often he'll employ these people as bridges to your destination, and doors of opportunity will open like never before. "Use all your skill to put me together; I wait to see your finished product" (Ps. 25:21).

Notes
1. Horatius Bonar, "Do You Rejoice in God's Sovereignty?" http://grace-for-today.com/590.htm.
2. Ibid.
3. Charles Swindoll, *Perfect Trust*, (Nashville TN: Thomas Nelson, 2000).

CHAPTER EIGHT

Making the Most of Your Pain

I'M LEAPING AND SINGING IN THE CIRCLE OF YOUR LOVE; YOU SAW MY PAIN, YOU DISARMED MY TORMENTORS.
PSALM 31:7

THESE ARE NOT DARK DAYS: THESE ARE GREAT DAYS—THE GREATEST DAYS OUR COUNTRY HAS EVER LIVED; AND WE MUST ALL THANK GOD THAT WE HAVE BEEN ALLOWED . . . TO PLAY A PART IN MAKING THESE DAYS MEMORABLE IN OUR HISTORY.[1]
WINSTON CHURCHILL

Most of us know people who have become angry, bitter, jealous or resentful while waiting for a divine delay to end. We've all known of godly Christians who have been stricken with a deadly disease; of brokenhearted women who have tried, unsuccessfully, to become pregnant; and of employees who have been continually passed over for a promotion. Yet deep within each of these scenarios are seeds of destiny that cannot survive if bathed in bitterness and pain.

Pain can actually become a powerful tool for uncovering the true nature of our heart. For example, if you've been passed over for an opportunity for advancement, the pain you experienced may have revealed that your heart was filled with pride, envy and jealously. Or perhaps you didn't get your own way in a situation and the pain of disappointment you felt revealed a heart of self-ishness within you. Like me, you are probably not proud of the times in your life when the pain of rejection revealed immaturi-ty. Yet these painful moments of self-discovery serve as a kind of looking glass, driving you to your knees in prayer because you don't like the image staring back at you.

Some of our most meaningful experiences in prayer will like-ly occur during our darkest days. But our heartfelt prayer can turn these times into some of our greatest days. When we allow our pain to give way to deep levels of prayer, God transforms us. The change occurs because we give up our desires in exchange for His. Desperation for *His* solution to the problem causes us to pray a "Whatever it takes, Lord" kind of prayer, even if it means giving up the object of our desire in exchange for knowing God on a deeper level.

In this season of waiting, we must learn that the pain of unanswered prayer can be a positive force. If handled properly, it can reshape our perspective and change the very nature of our thoughts and emotions. Pain can become positive when it directs us to reach deeper and more earnestly for God's greater plan for our life.

PRAY UNCONDITIONALLY

I've said that there is not much we can do to speed up the process of a divine delay. But I never said that there is *nothing* we can do. The book of 1 Samuel tells the story of a woman named Hannah who endured the intense emotional pain often associ-ated with a divine delay. Hannah turned her deep agony into a desperate appeal to God, and as a result, she won the battle over bitterness, anger and resentment. In the end, God used the burden of Hannah's heart to meet a surprisingly greater burden of His own heart—the birthing of a prophet to the nation, Samuel.[2]

Hannah was married to a man named Elkanah, who had two wives. Elkanah's second wife, Peninnah, had children, while Hannah did not. Every year, Elkanah took his family to a place called Shiloh to worship and offer a sacrifice to God. The Bible says that Peninnah taunted Hannah "cruelly, rubbing it in and never letting her forget that GOD had not given her children. This went on year after year. Every time she went to the sanctuary of GOD she could expect to be taunted. Hannah was reduced to tears and had no appetite" (1 Sam. 1:6-7).

Eli served as the priest of God at Shiloh. One day, he came upon Hannah in the Temple as she cried out to God. "In bitterness of soul Hannah wept much and prayed to the LORD. And she made a vow, saying, 'O LORD Almighty, if you will only look upon your servant's misery and remember me, and not forget your servant but give her a son, then I will give him to the LORD for all the days of his life'" (vv. 10-11, NIV). Eli then encouraged Hannah by saying, "Go in peace, and may the God of Israel grant you what you have asked of him" (v. 17, NIV).

God used the burden of Hannah's heart to bring a surprisingly larger solution to the burden of His own heart—the need to bring forth a prophet. Barrenness was not only Hannah's condition, but Israel's condition as well. Samuel was born during a season of spiritual need and scarce prophetic activity in Israel. God looked for a voice that would speak on His behalf to His people. Hannah did not know that her intense desire for a son was moving in concert with God's desire for an entire nation. As she entrusted the longings of her heart to God, He moved on her behalf, but He also advanced His larger plan.[3]

Yet I believe that Hannah was asking for more than just an answer to prayer. She had a deeper desire. In essence, she asked for the joy of knowing that God had not forgotten her. For Hannah, the affirmation of her relationship with God became more precious than anything else. In return, God blessed her with not one child, but several children. Hannah's pain was a prelude to the fulfillment of the promise of God.

Have you ever been so desperate for an answer to prayer that it didn't matter how God responded—just as long as He said or did *something*? Have you ever felt so desperate that your expectation for an answer was reduced to nothing and all you really wanted to know was that God heard your prayer? This is unconditional prayer. Its goal is an affirmation of your relationship with God. This affirmation produces within you a transformation of your self-worth—especially since it takes a huge beating while you are waiting for God.

Hannah became so desperate that she was willing to sacrifice the pleasure of keeping her son for the satisfaction of knowing that God had not forgotten her. She no longer had any hint of a selfish motive in how she prayed during her divine delay. Unconditional prayer demonstrates to God that He has complete ownership of our heart. Instead of our desires ruling our thoughts and emotions, God sits in the center of every chamber. Our love is not divided. Our focus is not distracted. Our heart is completely devoted to Him.

The bottom line is that when we pray an unconditional prayer to God, we basically say to Him, "God, I don't care about the benefit I will receive from the answer to this prayer. Please, take this situation and use it for your purpose. I'm

UNCONDITIONAL PRAYER DEMONSTRATES TO GOD THAT HE HAS COMPLETE OWNERSHIP OF OUR HEART.

happy to be used by you. Although my life is hidden in you, I need to know that I am not forgotten." We must realize that God sometimes wants to use our desires to facilitate His greater plan for our home, our job, our community or our church. He moves us to unconditional prayer so that His agenda is accomplished.

God wants to use you for a purpose greater than you can imagine. So don't be afraid to pray an unconditional prayer and, in return, get the affirmation of His affection. Give up ownership to the things God has promised you and let Him dictate how those things will be used. Do you have an inheritance or a legal settlement that's been held up for months or years? Tell God that you'll let Him have it. Have you asked God for healing so that you can do the kind of work you used to do? Tell Him that you'll go wherever He wants you to go and do whatever He wants you to do. Give Him your proverbial Samuel. Let the burden of your heart bring a surprisingly larger solution to the burden of His heart.

PRAY UNRESERVEDLY

Praying unreservedly is what I like to call "crying out" prayer. Throughout the Scriptures, men and women sought God for the things that *only* He could do. I'm sure that Hannah never dreamed she'd end up barren and with no one to turn to but God. Life rarely turns out the way we expect. Delayed promises seem easier to manage when we see them coming. But how often does that happen? The truth is that we seldom see disappointment approaching. It's always the treacherous assault beyond the horizon that we never anticipate. It's those mental muggings that we cannot see that buckle our knees. I'm sure that most of you know what I'm talking about. After the initial blow, we are left stunned and wondering what hit us.

Times such as these demand crying-out prayer. It's clear that God approves of unabashed petitions from us. The Bible tells us that even the psalmist engaged in this kind of prayer: "To the LORD I cry aloud, and he answers me from his holy hill" (Ps. 3:4, *NIV*). "I cry aloud to the LORD; I lift up my voice to the LORD for mercy" (Ps. 42:1, *NIV*). "Then they cried out to the LORD in their trouble, and he brought them out of their distress" (Ps. 107:28, *NIV*).

The strange thing is that sometimes God wants us to cry out to Him about a problem before He'll do anything about it. This is because it communicates our absolute dependence on His power. Crying out to God underscores our total helplessness and humility. And it is humility that moves the hand of God. Remember what James said: "Humble yourselves before the Lord, and he will lift you up" (Jas. 4:10, *NIV*).

In other words, God can lift us up when we have been put down by the vicissitudes of life. What would you do if your toddler fell down and bruised his knee? If it was just a tiny boo-boo, you'd probably tell little Johnny that he'd be all right. But if his pain was so intense that he cried out loudly, you'd come running to his rescue. Sometimes, God doesn't want us to just pray a little prayer, but to cry out in prayer. Then He'll come running.

David put it this way: "Evening and morning and at noon I will pray, and cry aloud, and He shall hear my voice" (Ps. 55:17, *NKJV*). The word "cry" in this verse is a Hebrew word that means "to make a loud sound"—even a growl or a roar.[4] Something powerful and supernatural happens when we cry out unreservedly to God. For most of my life, I assumed that crying out to God was just like other postures of prayer. I've come to learn, however, that the Bible teaches something different. Both the Old and New Testaments employ a variety of words to describe crying out in prayer or praying loudly. In each case, the meaning in these phrases includes some sort of audible sound—anything from a moan all the way to ear-splitting shouts.

Obviously, God is not hard of hearing. Everyone knows that He hears the faintest prayers spoken in the silence of our heart. But sometimes crying-out prayer is needed to engage our emotions and to help us pray more passionately. Why should we practice this kind of prayer? Well, passionate prayer has great power with God.

Maybe we're having a problem in our marriage or in our finances, but we haven't yet cried out loudly to God about it. God sees the problem and wants to work on it, but sometimes He will not work on a divine delay until first we say, "I've got to get alone somewhere where I can pray unreservedly to God." God sees our financial problems, but He may want us to become more concerned about it and to cry out before He does anything about it.

A solitary car ride makes a great location for crying out prayer. This is one of the places where I pray unabashedly and unreservedly when I can't find anyplace else to go. When I'm driving down the road, I don't worry about what people in the cars around me might think of my ravings. I'm sure they think I'm talking on a cell phone. They don't know that I'm actually talking to God.

A few years ago, Anthony, one of the pastors at our church, began having symptoms of a severe cold that was marked by an uncontrollable cough. When Anthony visited the doctor, he was shocked to discover that he was suffering from a rare, incurable and potentially fatal disease called sarcoidosis. This chronic illness is marked by the development of lesions in the lungs, bones, skin and eyes. Anthony's only option was to begin a treatment with a steroid called Prednisone. The doctors gave him little reason for optimism. "All you can do is take the medication and hope for the best," they told him.

However, Anthony used his painful experience as an opportunity to engage God in worship and prayer. He continued this practice despite the stream of bad news that kept coming in from his doctors. The next blow came when the steroids sent him on an emotional and physical roller-coaster ride. Soon, Anthony's days were filled with mood swings, headaches, weight gain, blurred vision and skin problems. Since he was scheduled to take the medication for an entire year, any hope of a normal future looked dim.

Nevertheless, Anthony was determined to keep up his regular routine. As he cried out in worship, he began to trust and believe in God for a divine healing. He was determined to allow his pain to turn him toward God. Yet despite his positive outlook, Anthony's condition continued to worsen. Some of his friends urged him to take a leave of absence from work, but Anthony refused to be defeated by his illness. After six months with no improvement, he began to struggle through bouts of anxiety and depression. At times, he wondered why it was taking so long for God to answer his prayers. Ironically, he prayed for other people suffering from various sicknesses and diseases during this time, and many of them were divinely healed while he continued to experience pain.

One day, Anthony opened his Bible and came across the words of Psalm 42:5: "Why are you downcast, O my soul? Put your hope in God." At that moment, he purposed in his heart to no longer succumb to depression regarding his unanswered prayers. Anthony began to look to God for a release from his trial. This psalm and others helped him to center his faith in God's ability to reign in his life. He learned to take his eyes off of his misery and direct them toward God.

From that point on, Anthony decided that no matter how he felt, he would believe God for his healing. Slowly, Anthony weaned himself off the Prednisone, and the symptoms of his disease began to disappear. Soon, his breathing returned to normal, and the fatigue and depression that he had lived with were lifted. The doctor was amazed by the change in Anthony's health.

Even the nurse who took his X-rays told him, "I see X-rays of people with your condition all the time. Sometimes, sarcoidosis goes into remission. When it does, you can see a scar on the lungs that shows that it is still there, but just lying dormant. However, your X-ray doesn't show anything at all! There's nothing there, not even a scar!" Anthony replied, "That's because the Lord healed me!"

ANOTHER SURPRISE ENDING

God is a master of surprise endings. I think He actually revels in reversals. The Bible says that He will even use the foolish things of this world to confound the wise. At the end of her challenge, Hannah sang a song celebrating God's great reversal in her life:

> He raises up the poor from the dust;
> he lifts the needy from the ash heap,
> to make them sit with princes
> and inherit a seat of honor.

> The Lord! His adversaries shall be shattered;
> the Most High will thunder in heaven.
> The Lord will judge the ends of the earth;
> he will give strength to his king,
> and exalt the power of his anointed (1 Sam. 2:8,10, NRSV).

Hannah could now rejoice after giving birth to the delayed promise. In the midst of her praise, she honed in on how God sometimes works through the most unlikely people to produce His will. And He does so by turning weakness to strength and by transforming death to life. In His infinite wisdom, God lifts seemingly insignificant people to places of power and brings the prideful down to the dust.

Hannah's song also shows that God's choice is not always man's choice. Remember the selection process of David as king? David was just a poor shepherd boy who was nearly forgotten about during the selection process for king because he was out in the fields tending the animals. Thankfully, God judges us by our insides, though man looks on the outside.

YOUR PAIN CAN MAKE YOU POWERFUL

I believe that the pain of a divine delay can be a powerfully positive force, though we usually don't view pain this way. Each of us has experienced bouts of pain that propelled us into doubt, discouragement, depression or despair. Perhaps you are having this kind of response to your pain right now. But, since you cannot change the pain, why not change your perspective of it? Why not change the way you respond to your pain?

Someone once said that pain is inevitable, but misery is optional. Misery and bitterness are choices. If we are miserable today, we have most likely chosen misery over other options. If we are bitter, it is most likely because we have rehearsed our past hurts over and over in our minds. Maybe we did not know about other options, because our pain blinded us from having hope.

Changing our perspective about our pain isn't easy, but it does work! It works when we pray unconditionally, unselfishly and unreservedly. It all depends on us. We can choose to run from the pain. We can choose to whine about it. We can choose

MISERY AND BITTERNESS ARE CHOICES. IF WE ARE MISERABLE TODAY, WE HAVE MOST LIKELY CHOSEN MISERY OVER OTHER OPTIONS.

to waste it. We can even choose to deny the reality of it. It really is up to us. But if we want to become powerful, we must choose to embrace our pain in prayer.

That's right. In order for our pain to become a powerfully positive force in our life, we must take ownership of it. We can't blame it on someone else. We have to hold it close and be determined to let it go only when we're able to fully acknowledge the good it's working in us, through us and for us. We must be able to look that pain smack in the face, grab it by the shoulders, and call it our friend. And we have to do this without a hint of bitterness or self-pity.

Making the most of pain requires that we wrap our arms—flabby biceps and all—around the thing that is working us into a frenzy. The only way to do this is through prayer. For now, remember two mottos: First, "Nothing is wasted in God's economy." The events leading up to a miracle are just as significant as the miracle itself. Second, "Whatever doesn't kill us will eventually make us stronger." Together, these two sayings can bring meaning to our misery. Together, they signify that every painful, crushing, devastating or disappointing experience that we experience has value beyond the pain they ultimately cause.

I'm at a season in life where my past is being put into a wonderful new perspective. Even things that currently cause me pain are beginning to look more like blessings instead of bruises. I now know that God often allows us to experience pain in preparation for some future pleasure. I have discovered that a new day will dawn—a new morning will come!

Morning Will Come

How can I bear the pain?
So many plans . . . permanently interrupted
So many dreams shattered

Hopes . . . dashed
All gone . . . Why?
Why this? Why now? Why me?
Helplessness . . . hopelessness
Life will never be the same again
Is it even worth living?

Where are you, God?

I'm right here beside you, my child.
Even though you may not feel my presence,
I'm holding you close under the shadow of my wings
I will walk with you through this dark night.

Do not shrink from weeping
I gave you tears for emotional release
Don't try to hide your grief
Let it become for you a source of healing
A process of restoration
For I have planned it so
Those who mourn shall be blessed
I'll be holding on to you
Even when you feel you can't hold on to me.

Seek my face
Receive my promise, impossible as it may seem now
That joy will come in the morning
It may take much time
But, I will heal your broken heart.
I know the night seems endless,
But morning will come
I have promised.

—Author Unknown

SURVIVAL SECRETS
Remember

The Picture from the Past: Pray unconditionally and unselfishly, because God has not forgotten you.

The Practice for the Present: Pray unreservedly, because in the end you will be rewarded with God's unfailing love.

The Promise for the Future: "He raises up the poor from the dust and lifts the needy from the ash heap; he seats them with princes and has them inherit a throne of honor" (1 Sam. 2:8, *NIV*).

Notes
1. *The Oxford Dictionary of Quotations* (London, England: Oxford University Press, Edition, 1953), p. 144:7.
2. Jane Hansen, *Fashioned for Intimacy: Reconciling Men and Women to God's Original Design* (Ventura, CA: Regal Books, 1997).
3. Ibid.
4. Bill Gothard, *The Power of Crying Out* (Sisters, OR: Multnomah Publishers, 2002).
5. Ibid.

Are We There Yet?

PRAISE BE TO THE NAME OF GOD FOR
EVER AND EVER; WISDOM AND POWER ARE HIS.
HE CHANGES TIMES AND SEASONS.
DANIEL 2:20-21, *NIV*

When our children were young, my husband and I sometimes took them on day trips. Early in the morning, while the dew was still on the grass, we'd all pile into our car and head for a nearby pool, aquarium or other play spot. We'd return later that day, exhausted from our mini-vacation. During those times, our daughters, Danielle and Jessica, spent many hours in the back of our car singing, coloring, sleeping and complaining.

Usually, within the first 10 minutes of the trip, Danielle and Jessica would become restless and begin the incessant whining mantra of, "Are we there yet?" In the book of Acts, the disciples asked the resurrected Jesus a similar question: "Are you going to restore the kingdom to Israel now? Is this the time?" (Acts 1:6). Little did they know that they were merely at the beginning of a very long journey. Listen to the way Jesus answered their question regarding the issue of God's timing:

You don't get to know the time. Timing is the Father's business. What you'll get is the Holy Spirit. And when the Holy Spirit comes on you, you will be able to be my witnesses in Jerusalem, all over Judea and Samaria, even to the ends of the world (Acts 1:7-8).

Don't you just love the way Jesus responds to thorny questions? I wish I could get out of sticky situations with His kind of wisdom and grace. There is a particular timelessness about God that leaves us groping around to make sense of His dealings. If the Lord had answered with an outright, "No," those poor, weary and confused disciples probably would have given up hope. Instead, the Master issued a challenge for His friends to recognize that timing is the Father's business.

GOD IS NOT HELD CAPTIVE BY TIME

Sometimes, we think that God—the Almighty, omniscient and omnipotent Father—can be moved when we point impatiently to our wristwatches. Well, we don't actually point to our watches, but we communicate this same message to God by constantly worrying about tomorrow. When we are convinced that it's taking too long to get where we want to go, we begin to doubt God's ability to work on our behalf by relegating it to our own understanding of time. We foolishly try to tie God to our human timeframes and schedules. Then, when He doesn't fall in line with our timing, we panic.

I have news for you. God is greater than the limitations of our clock or calendar. He is ageless, ceaseless, endless and perpetual. He is not held captive by time. Psalm 90:1-4 says:

God, it seems you've been our home forever; long before the mountains were born, long before you brought earth itself to birth, from "once upon a time" to "kingdom come"—you are God. So don't return us to mud, saying,

"Back to where you came from!" Patience! You've got all the time in the world—whether a thousand years or a day, it's all the same to you.

It's a good thing that God is different from us. He can (and does) move outside of our expectations, deadlines and timelines. Jesus' statement to the apostles in Acts 1:7-8 confirms that the Father has power over time and can use it to achieve His purposes. Again and again, we see that the future belongs to God. Yet, most of us don't want to accept this fact. We are creatures bound by time and held captive to the mystery of the future.

Yet the dealings of God are not necessarily bound by time. So, in our season of delay, it is not wise to become overly preoccupied with God's timing. Simply put, we can't control God's schedule. Although this creates some tension between the issues of God's sovereignty and the effects of our free will, the bottom line is this: The only result that comes from worrying about God's timing is stress, tiredness and even sickness.

Daniel 2:21 declares that God "changes times and seasons" (*NIV*). Since God doesn't always tell us when He'll bring His promises to pass, it might be wise to stop bugging Him with such questions as, "Lord, when are You going to change my husband? When will I get that job or find a wife? When will revival come to my city and nation? At what point will my life take on greater significance and satisfaction? Lord, what about my healing? When, when, when?"

OUR JOB IS TO KEEP AN OPEN EAR TO THE SPIRIT OF GOD
SO THAT WE CAN RECOGNIZE WHEN THE WINDS OF CHANGE
ARE BEGINNING TO BLOW IN OUR LIFE.

Forgive my bluntness, but timing is the Father's business, not ours! Our job is to keep an open ear to the Spirit of God so that we can recognize when the winds of change are beginning to blow in our life.

I believe the question most of us really want to ask is not necessarily why God waits but how *can* He wait. How can He restrain Himself from coming to our rescue when we are hurting or when we're suffering? How can He wait so long before turning the tide of our tragedy? How can He delay when we have reached the end of our hopes?

Most people do things based on their background, their personality traits or just in response to a pressing need. But we all act according to our individual make-up. Each of us is different from anyone else in the world, so we respond to situations in different ways. Similarly, the question of why God waits can be answered when we take an intimate look at His uniqueness. Immediately, we find that God is very different from us.

Throughout Christian history, men and women have often referred to God's uniqueness as the "otherness" of God. Otherness speaks of the transcendent quality of God, which, in some ways, establishes distance between us and Him. This otherness points to God's absolute priority above created entities. He is not like us. In Isaiah 55:8, God Himself states, "I don't think the way you think. The way you work isn't the way I work."

The thought of God as "other" is crucial. God is immutable and impassable. He is spirit, and thus is like no other being known to man. That puts God and His otherness into a category outside humanity's ability to fully understand it. But we can make every effort to become more sensitive and aware of God's otherness. Developing this kind of sensitivity and awareness is at the heart of knowing why God waits. It is like tuning our antennae to receive God at maximum signal.

Since God is timeless and sovereign, what attitude *should* we have regarding our ticking timer? In Ephesians 5:16, the apostle Paul encourages us by saying, "These are evil times, so make every minute count" (*CEV*). Paul tells us that we are to strategically make use of each and every day—even our days of waiting.

BECOME A GOOD STEWARD OF YOUR TIME

I believe that it was Benjamin Franklin who said, "Dost thou love life? Then do not squander time, for that is the stuff life is made of." Our responsibility is to spend time focusing on the stuff life is made of. These are such things as serving God, promoting the gospel, doing good to others, and finding joy in this journey. The author of Hebrews made this mandate clear when he said, "Keep your eyes on Jesus, who both began and finished this race we're in. Study how he did it. Because he never lost sight of where he was headed—that exhilarating finish in and with God—he could put up with anything along the way: cross, shame, whatever" (Heb. 12:2).

Christians who are good stewards of their time do what Jesus did: They focus on where they're going. They consistently keep their priorities straight by running their lives (with God's direction and help) according to the things that are most important to the Father. This means living by the practice of putting their relationship with God first, their relationships with others second, and their responsibilities third.

We live in a society that demands that we accomplish everything—today. As a result, we often lose our focus on being good stewards of our time. Technology is racing to make us do more than we've ever done before. Too often, the really important things get left out of the schedule.

In his book *The 7 Habits of Highly Effective People*, Steven R. Covey asks, "Is getting more things done in less time going to make a difference, or will it just increase the pace at which I react to the people and circumstances that seem to control my life? Could there be something I need to see in a deeper, more fundamental way—some paradigm within myself that affects the way I see my time, my life, and my own nature?"[1]

Many years ago, I heard a story about a very wise man who understood how to cultivate a deeper appreciation for each day. He was an expert in time management and regularly held a class for a group of business students. One day as he stood in front of his class of high-powered overachievers, he said, "Okay, it's time for a quiz." He pulled out an over-sized, wide-mouth mason jar and set it on the desk in front of him. Then he reached under a table and pulled out about a dozen fist-sized rocks and carefully placed them, one at a time, into the jar.

When the jar was filled to the brim, he asked the class, "Is the jar full?" Everyone in the class yelled, "Yes!"

"Really?" the time management expert replied. He reached under the table and pulled out a bucket of gravel. He dumped some gravel into the jar and shook it, causing the pieces of gravel to work themselves down into the spaces between the rocks.

He then asked the group once more, "Is the jar full?" By this time, the class was on to his point—or so they thought. "Probably not," one of them answered.

"Good!" he replied. He reached under the table and brought out a bucket of sand. He started dumping the sand in the jar, which went into all the spaces left between the rocks and the gravel. Once more he asked the question, "Is the jar full?" "No!" the class shouted.

"Good!" he said. He grabbed a pitcher of water and poured the water into the jar until the jar was filled to the brim. Then he looked at the class and asked, "What is the point of this illustration?"

One eager beaver raised his hand and said, "The point is that no matter how full your schedule is, if you try really hard, you can always fit some more things in it!"

"No," the speaker replied. "That's not the point. The truth that this illustration teaches us is that if you don't put the big rocks in first, you'll never get them in at all."

One student asked, "What do you really mean by the term 'big rocks'?"

The man answered, "They represent the time spent with your loved ones; the time spent investing in your faith, your education, your dreams; or the time spent performing a worthy cause such as teaching or mentoring others. Remember to put these big rocks in first, or you'll never get them in at all."

As you reflect on this short story, ask yourself the question: What are the big rocks in my life? And then, put those—the most important things—in your schedule first. Recognize God's timing in this waiting season. It is a time to invest in your priorities. A life well lived is built on time well spent.

COOPERATE WITH GOD'S TIMING

In order to cooperate with God's timing, we must be willing to let Him make necessary changes inside of us. He may want to give us a passion for something very different from what we've pursued in the past. Passion is the ability to feel deeply and reach widely. And I believe that this emotion exists in all of us.

I'm sorry to say this but many people lose touch with this part of themselves as they wait for God. I'm sure that you know what I'm talking about. I can almost hear you saying, "I've had the everlasting aspirations knocked out of me long ago." But God knows how to get those aspirations back into your heart. This kind of passionate living will make you do things that you wouldn't otherwise dream of doing. It will put you into situations that you would rather avoid. Sometimes, it will even completely change the direction of your life.

Since his childhood, my husband, David, wanted to be an engineer. He and his two brothers devoured every copy of *Popular Mechanics* magazine that their dad brought home. As soon as they were old enough to work a screwdriver, they began taking apart everything in the house to see if they could put it back together and make it work again. At age 16, David entered college on a partial athletic scholarship to study engineering. Throughout his college years, he had been a skeptic and persecutor of Christians. Then suddenly, two months after graduating with a bachelor's degree in mechanical engineering, he gave his life to Jesus Christ.

In the fall of that same year, David began a master's program in civil engineering. Moved by the joy of his newfound faith, he immediately became an evangelist on campus and a man of faith and prayer. With six months left before graduation, his foremost prayer was that God would help him find just the right job as a civil engineer.

Armed with a grade point average of 3.6 and the prestige of having a full academic scholarship, David felt that he really did not have to pray for a job. He expected to have his pick of the litter. However, a month or two went by, and no job offers came in. Although he had been invited to an impressive number of interviews, he had not received a single offer. David began to feel the pressure, so he boldly said, "Lord, if You will give me a job in my field, I'll give You 10 percent of everything I earn."

Three months before graduation, David still had no job. So he decided to sweeten the offer by upping the ante to 15 percent. David now knows that it is useless and doctrinally incorrect to attempt to bribe God, but as a young Christian, the proposal made perfect sense to him. By the time graduation day came, he had upped the ante to 20 percent. Yet he still had not received any job offers in his field.

Shortly after graduation, David finally landed a job—at a spaghetti factory. For eight hours each day, he would stand on a 30-foot platform dropping spaghetti down a chute. It was the only job he could find. Every other door he knocked on had been slammed in his face. He had sent out resumes to hundreds of engineering companies from New Jersey to Saudi Arabia, yet every company he applied to had turned him down.

Of course, David's classmates were stepping into great engineering jobs despite having little or no faith, less experience, and lower GPAs than David had. It was as though God was resisting him at every turn. Finally, David realized that God was trying to teach him something. He had used every trick he knew of to avoid this lesson from God, but he simply couldn't escape the fact that once God gets you in His vise grip, there's no use in struggling to get out.

Eventually, David left the spaghetti factory to take a better-paying job. At that point, the only job he could find was at Clairol—not in the corporate offices, but in a factory, sorting bottles of hair spray into boxes and then dumping the boxes into labeling chutes. By this time, David was emotionally vacillating between making bold confessions of faith for the "real" job that he longed for and drowning in the depths of despair because of the very real job that he had.

One day, it all came to a head when David went out to sit in his old beat-up jalopy during his lunch break. Sitting in that car was depressing enough, but what added to his despair was that he didn't have any food at home to make lunch, and he didn't have any money to buy lunch. He pulled out his pocket New Testament and began to read. The more he read, the angrier he became. He cried out, "Look at what God says about Himself in His Word—and look at the job I am doing!"

David then began to pray. Actually, he was arguing with God. "God, this is not right!" he yelled as the tears rolled down his cheeks, the anger welled up in his heart, and his mind filled with disappointment. He was screaming at the top of his lungs as he sat in the Clairol factory parking lot with the windows rolled up. People must have thought he had gone over the edge. They were probably right.

That day, for the first time in his life, the Holy Spirit spoke to David with crystal clarity. "David," He said, "If I call you to work in this job for the rest of your life, will you do it?" David answered, "Yes, if that is Your plan for me, that is what I will do."

David experienced a real breakthrough in his life that day. In the short time he had been a Christian, he had considered a job in civil engineering to be God's promise and the answer to his prayers. That day in the car, he didn't know if he would ever work a day in his life as an engineer. Yet though he didn't know what God was calling him to do and he didn't get the job he had hoped for, David received something even better that day—the knowledge that God would bring about whatever He had in mind for his life.

Today, my husband says, "Sometimes we become angry and frustrated with God because things do not work out the way we think they should or as quickly as we would like. I had my one-year, three-year, and five-year plans, but God scrubbed my plans so that He could work something in me that He wanted. Although I didn't realize it back then, God was positioning me to serve others."

Yet David's delay was not all about his needs. He eventually practiced civil engineering in the consulting engineering field for seven years, until God revealed the next step in His promise for him. But during his time in engineering, he held his career loosely and with more humility than he would have if God hadn't taken him through this process of giving him a passion for joyfully serving—no matter what the job. That day, my sweetheart's passion for engineering was transformed into a passion for service.

In order to cooperate with God's timing, we need to have passion—a desire that gets us up in the morning and that challenges and catapults us beyond our self-imposed limitations. Without such a passion, we simply wade around in the stagnant waters of life. With it, however, we open ourselves to one of the most basic elements of a vibrant and fruitful expression of our faith—the plan and the will of God.

RECOGNIZE GOD'S TIMING

Isn't it funny how little children have a poor sense of time and space? Most of them don't know the difference between a 10-minute ride and a 2-hour trip. Oh, how much easier parenting would be if we did not have to answer that irritating and often repeated question, "What time is it?" Then moms and dads all over the world could stop pulling out their hair.

To tell the truth, most of us don't have a sense of timing within our own divine delay. However, we should work to understand the God season we're in. The Bible tells us that we need to know when we're in a God season so that we don't miss our miracle moment. Jesus said, "You know how to interpret the appearance of the earth and the sky. How is it that you don't know how to interpret this present time?" (Luke 12:55, *NIV*).

There are at least two kinds of time indicated in the Bible: *chronos* time and *kairos* time. Chronos (or chronological) time is what we get by looking at our clocks and calendars—seconds,

IN ORDER TO COOPERATE WITH GOD'S TIMING, WE NEED TO HAVE PASSION—A DESIRE THAT CHALLENGES AND CATAPULTS US BEYOND OUR SELF-IMPOSED LIMITATIONS.

minutes, hours and years. Most of us pay attention to chronos time. Kairos time, on the other hand, refers to opportune times—the seasons of fresh and strategic opportunities in our lives.[2]

Our actions and attitudes in the chronos times of preparing, sowing, believing and persevering determine whether God can shift us into kairos time. For example, when I was pregnant, it could be said that I had nine months to carry my unborn child. The duration represented by those nine months is an example of chronos time. However, the moment my water broke and I told David, "It's time," I moved into kairos time—opportune time.

It has been said that we buy our life with each second of time we spend on Earth. I believe that our limited time on Earth is one of God's greatest gifts to us. When a chronos season is used wisely, God can move us into a fuller experience of His purpose and plan. Galatians 4:4 says, "But when the fullness of the time [kairos] had come, God sent forth His Son, born of a woman" (*NKJV*). God uses chronos to His honor and glory as a period of preparation for the more strategic kairos seasons. In his book *God's Timing for Your Life,* author Dutch Sheets writes:

> When we're in a non-strategic general season of life's daily routine plodding along in the chronos of time, God doesn't totally start over . . . His overall agenda does not change. He simply takes us through one phase of a process in which our perseverance and faithfulness have allowed him to shift us into the next phase of a strategic season. He changes the times and the seasons.[3]

The apostle Paul confirms this truth when he states, "Let us not lose heart and grow weary and faint in acting nobly and doing right, for in due time and at the appointed [kairos] season we shall reap, if we do not loosen and relax our courage and faint" (Gal. 6:9, *AMP*).

When we boil it all down, kairos refers to those unique times in our lives when we are presented with an opportunity for major change. These seasons are so awesome because an instant of ordinary time is transformed forever and a specific moment in the present becomes, quite literally, eternal. As the writer of 2 Peter 3:8 reminds us, "Do not ignore this one fact, beloved, that with the Lord one day is like a thousand years, and a thousand years are like one day" (*NAB*).

THE FIVE SIGNS OF A GOD SEASON

How do you know when you're about to enter a strategic kairos time? Just as there are indicators of the seasons of the year, there are signs that help us to know where we are on the continuum of God's timing. By reflecting on my past, I can see at least five signs that have helped me to recognize when a shift in God's timing is about to take place.

1. We Encounter an Extended Season of Waiting

Before we can enter into a strategic kairos time, we must first complete the prerequisites of handling our spiritual and natural responsibilities well. This includes

- continuing to wait patiently, but expectantly, for the Lord
- continuing to believe, live an honorable life, and be obedient
- consistently doing good to others

2. We Have a Unique Experience with God

Abraham and Sarah were visited by the three angelic strangers just before they conceived Isaac; Zechariah and Elizabeth were visited by the angel Gabriel prior to the conception of John the Baptist; and the disciples and the apostle Paul also had encounters with the supernatural just before God shifted the seasons in their lives. I believe that God still uses angels to prepare our hearts for the arrival of His divine timing. However, I don't think that we should go looking for a heavenly being to speak to us. More often than not, God will speak to us through the still, small voice of the Spirit; through providential circumstances; through dreams; or through other people as He prepares us for the shift from chronos to kairos times.

3. Fulfillment of a Promise or Dream in Our Life Seems Impossible

If you're like me, holding on to the promises of God after the fifth, tenth or (God forbid), twentieth year of waiting is tough. Yet history reminds us that the phrase "too late" is not in God's vocabulary. Even though our desire for the promise has aged beyond recognition, entering kairos times can occur out of the blue.

4. We Receive a New Perspective on Old Issues

We'll know that we're close to the end of our delay when it's easier than ever to have a deep appreciation for longstanding and difficult issues in our life. We'll no longer see certain problems as hurtful or a hindrance to a fruitful life. Instead, we'll see how integral our life is to the lives of those around us. We'll observe, as if for the first time, how much others need our love, mercy and grace. We'll become a great blessing to others—even the problem people in our life. You know the folks I'm talking about—they are the ones who always give us reasons to repent for our wrong words and wrong attitudes. We'll have a great desire to pray for them and show them kindness. These things will happen because it will be our season (see Ps. 1:3) and because our spiritual fruit has ripened and is ready to be picked.

5. Our Attachment to Material Possessions Begins to Diminish

For many of us, letting go of our favorite things is hard because we tend to connect our sense of worth to our most prized possessions. During one pre-kairos season in my life, God led me to give away some very sentimental belongings. It began by God telling me to give away a few of my most treasured Christmas decorations. Several years earlier, I'd purchased some decorative gift boxes covered with beautiful plush velvet fabric. I had never seen anything like them before. I'm almost embarrassed to say that each holiday season, I painstakingly arranged them under my tree and then sat back to admire their beauty and my interior decorating "skillz." The items were inexpensive, but for some reason I cherished them as if they could never be replaced.

As silly as it may seem, I wrestled with the Lord for two days over those stupid little red boxes. However, almost immediately after I obeyed God, I experienced an unexpected blessing. As soon as the boxes were out of my hands, a peculiar sense of pleasure swept over my entire being. Like a wave of the sea, I sensed the fresh contentment of a heart that had no attachment to the things of this world. Sure, through the years I'd given away hundreds of gifts to people, but not necessarily the things that were dear to my heart—not the items that held sentimental value to me.

From that moment on, I was like an addict, hooked to living sacrificially. It launched me into a deeper gratitude for God's unselfish Gift to humanity. In that season, I pledged to keep my heart pure from the entanglement of material wealth by regularly giving away more and more of my favorite things.

God wants to liberate our hearts from anything that tries to separate us from Him and His love. He also wants to prepare us for deeper and deeper realms of service to others. In the days leading up to your kairos season, expect some desires and struggles to fall off your soul like leaves off a tree. It may be a sign that you are right at the threshold of entering into the fullness of His promise for you.

TAKE YOUR EYES OFF THE CLOCK

Have you ever worked with clock-watchers? These are folks who can't wait for the workday to end so that they can pack up and go home. All day long, they check to see if it is time to leave. As a result, their work is mediocre and their employer is cheated out of an honest day's labor. What a huge waste of precious time, opportunities and resources.

I believe that one of the best things we can do during a season of waiting is to take our eyes off the clock. In doing so, we'll free our mind and heart to wait expectantly for God. The days are too short and God's benefits are too great to squander even one minute watching the hands of time go round and round. We need to take our eyes off the clock and trust God to bring a harvest of fruitfulness in our life.

Remember that in Acts 1:7-8, Jesus told His disciples to be busy for Him instead of being preoccupied with God's timing. He gave them a purpose and a reason to live. Their city, region and the world were crying out for a continued glimpse of Christ Jesus. Peter, James, John and the other disciples needed to continue the work that Jesus began. In the same way, Christ commissions us to go out and make a dynamic difference in the lives of those around us. Living the Christian life is not so much about what *Jesus* is going to do than it is about what He wants *us* to do while we wait for His return. It's more about us increasing the gospel's influence than about us waiting for our future rewards.

Jesus' disciples needed His assurance of their continued usefulness, and He gave it to them. We need that same assurance of our usefulness and fruitfulness in our own lives. And He gives it to us as well. His command to us is the same that it was for them: Go change the world!

I honestly believe that when we take care of God's business, He'll take care of ours. So what should we do about the passing of time? Wait and put our trust in the timeless and eternal God. He was with the disciples, and He'll be with us, too.

Oh, and if you're wondering how I answered my children when they asked, "Are we there yet?" I simply said to them, "No, we're not there yet. I'm driving and I'll let you know when we get close. For now, just sit back. Keep on doing what you're doing—enjoy the ride."

SURVIVAL SECRETS
Remember

The Picture from the Past: It is our responsibility to recognize God's timing, but not to try to change it. "Timing is the Father's business" (Acts 1:8).

The Practice for the Present: We need to put the "big rocks" in first or we'll never get them in at all.

The Promise for the Future: "Let the name of God be honored forever and ever, for wisdom and power belong to Him. He changes the times and the years. He takes kings away, and puts kings in power. He gives wisdom to wise men and much learning to men of understanding" (Dan. 2:20-21, *NLV*).

Notes

1. Steven Covey, *The 7 Habits of Highly Effective People* (New York: Simon and Schuster, 1989).
2. Dutch Sheets, *God's Timing For Your Life* (Ventura, CA: Regal Books, 2001).
3. Ibid.

CHAPTER TEN

The Future Belongs to God

THERE IS SURELY A FUTURE HOPE FOR YOU, AND YOUR HOPE WILL NOT BE CUT OFF.
PROVERBS 23:18, *NIV*

God GIVES A HAND TO THOSE DOWN ON THEIR LUCK, GIVES A FRESH START TO THOSE READY TO QUIT.
PSALM 145:14

While it is true that the future is not ours, God stands in that future, drawing us forward into destiny and eternity with Him. He always goes before us and then waits somewhere in the distant beyond. But He doesn't open the door for us to follow until He is thoroughly ready—until the appointed time. At that divine moment, He calls and beckons us to follow in His footsteps. Until then, He equips us to wait.

If the future belongs to God, we can trust that it is sure and secure. It may be beyond our grasp, but it's not beyond His. In the meantime, God is creating significant opportunities and outcomes all around us. So we need to wait for Him and not rush through life. This is the only way to *really* live.

We need to make sure that we're not missing out on seeing the Lord of today by only worshiping the Lord of tomorrow.

They're one and the same. And even when waiting causes the apparent death of our dreams, we need to trust God to turn our situation around. He has the power to resurrect dead things and to open our eyes to a grand view of His dealings in our life. Right now, we're learning to live life to the fullest, and that's what God wants us to do. But some day, a turning point will come.

This was never truer than in the life of Lazarus and his two sisters, Mary and Martha. When Lazarus became deathly ill, Jesus intentionally postponed coming to the aid of His friend. For four days, Mary and Martha waited for Jesus to come and heal their brother. John 11:5-7 gives us a glimpse of what happened: "Jesus loved Martha and her sister and Lazarus, but oddly, when he heard that Lazarus was sick, he stayed on where he was."

It's so amazing how the Lord intentionally orchestrated this drama. Look at what happened: Jesus was late—*intentionally* late. He *intentionally* allowed something devastating to happen. Unbeknownst to everyone else, Jesus was acting in love, and He knew exactly what He was doing. In the same way, sometimes God allows losses in our lives to occur—losses that He eventually uses to reveal His Lordship to us *and* to an unbelieving generation. Before going to heal Lazarus, Jesus told the disciples, "Lazarus is dead, and for your sake I am glad I was not there, so that you may believe" (John 11:14-15).

The Bible tells us that Lazarus was already in the tomb when Jesus made His grand entrance. He took charge of the funeral and told the mourners to take away the stone. Martha was afraid to do what Jesus had asked. She understood that dead things have an awful stench. Little did she know that the fragrance of God's goodness was about to be released *through* the act of Christ raising her brother from the dead.

Jesus shouted three words: "Lazarus, come forth." Through some supernatural means, Lazarus heard the call and rose to life. He responded by doing exactly what Jesus commanded: He walked out of the tomb. I believe that God is waiting to do the same thing for us. At the right time, the kairos time, He'll call us forward to live again. But our new life will be marked by the presence of His resurrection power and the fragrance of His goodness.

In the end, Martha and Mary got what they wanted, and God got what He wanted. The people of Judea were propelled into a new revelation of Christ's lordship. The Bible says that many believed in Him as a result of this miracle (see John 11:45). A reversal of tangible reality is possible when Christ is intent on helping us come to terms with His deity. God *can* use the demise of some aspect of our lives to give us a turnaround—a fresh start. If the future belongs to God, then in some ways the present belongs to us.

THE PROMISE OF GOD'S RESURRECTION POWER

I want to tell you the story of a woman I've chosen to call Samantha. By all accounts, she should not be alive today. Her future seemed to be ruined by a past filled with heartbreak and unimaginable tragedy. Yet today she stands strong and tall, with only a few unseen battle scars remaining from a time gone by.

Samantha's story begins when she was between the ages of 10 and 15. At that time, she was sexually molested by four different relatives. Like other victims of abuse, she never told anyone, because she didn't think anyone would believe her. What's more, because she came from a broken home, she felt that she

GOD *CAN* USE THE DEMISE OF SOME ASPECT OF OUR LIVES TO
GIVE US A TURNAROUND—A FRESH START.

had somehow invited the criminal abuse she received from her molesters. Life was like a painful sore that would not heal—an existence that seemed to end before it began.

As a young woman, Samantha had many failed relationships. She married prior to graduating from college in the hopes of settling down and raising a family of her own. But it wasn't long before she was devastated by the ultimate rejection—her husband ran off with another woman. After college, she met and married another man who promised to give her the love and security she craved. But the relationship was filled with affairs and abuse. In addition, he physically abused Samantha while she was pregnant. She and her unborn babies should have died, but they somehow survived.

The troubled couple visited a marriage counselor, but things didn't change. Samantha finally divorced her second husband and began the difficult task of letting God fill up all the empty places in her heart. She confessed, "I had given up on ever being what God had called me to be and ever having a whole family. My dreams were nearly dead, and my hopes of ever having the family I wanted were nearly dead as well."

One day, Samantha asked God why her life reeked with the smell of tragedy. God seldom tells us all of the reasons why things go wrong in our lives, but He gave Samantha two important thoughts to hold on to. First, the Lord helped her to see that one day she'd be able to comfort and help other women who had been abused in the way that she had. Second, He held before her the promise of His resurrection power. Samantha shared that "God impressed on my heart that some situations have to be Lazarus dead [in the grave for four days, stinking with the insides rotting] before they can be resurrected."

Inwardly, Samantha's heart and hopes seemed to die many times while she waited for things to change. But little by little, through prayer, worship and studying God's Word, she began to respond to the call of "Samantha, come forth!" Moment by moment, this remarkable woman learned to live despite the factors working against her. Her secret was an incredible ability to continue waiting for God.

I met with Samantha on a regular basis, and together we believed God for a miracle to take place in her life. In a short period of time, she remarried. Samantha's new husband works in full-time ministry and treats her like a queen. Today, Samantha can confidently say that God does speak new life into dead things. She has been healed and freed from the wounds of her past. Today, she wouldn't trade what she has for anything in the world. She is alive again because she waited on God and His resurrection power.

THERE IS LIFE AFTER DEATH

When time and circumstances cause the devastation of divorce, finances to dry up, children to act up, or dreams to be delayed, we need to trust that God has the power to resurrect us and give us a new beginning. Resurrection life is not just for the future; it is also for today. In his book *God's Power is for You*, author Dr. Wesley Duewel writes:

> Resurrection power for the Christian is not primarily spectacular power to *do*; it is God's amazing power to enable us to *be*. God wants our life to be a demonstration of the very same power of the Holy Spirit that raised Christ from the dead. He doesn't want our life to manifest spiritual defeat and to carry about the smell of death; He wants our life to manifest abundance, victory, and glory—to manifest the sweet fragrance and aroma of Christ wherever we go (see 2 Cor. 2:14-15). He wants our daily life to be a living demonstration of the world's greatest miracle—His resurrection power.[1]

Paul testified about how this aspect of God's grace worked in his own life (see Eph. 3:20; Col. 1:29). And look at how the Psalmist prayed for resurrection power: "Why not help us make a fresh start—a resurrection life? Then your people will laugh and sing" (Ps. 85:6). In Zechariah 10:6, God says, "I'll put muscle in the people of Judah; I'll save the people of Joseph. I know their pain and will make them good as new. They'll get a fresh start, as if nothing had ever happened. And why? Because I am their very own GOD, I'll do what needs to be done for them." These Scriptures teach us how to effectively pray for and hope in God's awesome, miracle-working power. As one man put it, "The resurrection gives my life meaning and direction and the opportunity to start over no matter what my circumstances."

DON'T MISS YOUR MIRACLE

Most people know that dead men tell no tales. Well, I believe that God's resurrection power causes things that were previously dead to tell great tales. They tell of a God who can roll back the hands of time. They testify of a God who can actually reverse the reality of lost opportunities. They tell of a God who can bring good out of tragedy—of a God who still does miracles. But when the miracle takes place, *it* tells the ultimate tale—that we serve a God who is all-powerful and who holds our future in His hands.

Yet if we're not careful, we'll miss out on the miraculous power of God during our delay. This is a time when the Lord wants to use us to prove His supremacy. Some of us might say, "God doesn't need to prove anything to anybody." That is absolutely right. He doesn't *need* to prove it, but He does it anyway. Why? He does it to teach us about His character and nature. The miracles in the Bible are there to teach us that God can do *anything*. They remind us to expect miracles in our own lives. But we can miss our miracle by expecting things to happen in an instant—especially when God sometimes does the miraculous in His own timing and at His own pace.

Most of us expect speedy or instantaneous miracles. We expect a miracle to solve our financial challenges and begin to look for a check for one million dollars in the mail, or for a big promotion at work, or for some other financial windfall. We expect a miraculous healing to occur after only one prayer is prayed. We wait for God to instantaneously restore our marriage, although it took decades for the love to wear away.

I see at least two kinds of miracles in the Bible: those that happen when someone asks for it, and those that happen in God's timing. What miraculous thing is God attempting to do in your life that you may be missing because you expect it to happen in your timing? What does God want to do in your marriage, your church, your finances, your family, or your career? What does He want to do in your heart or with your health? Whatever God wants to do for you, I'd like to be the first to tell you this: Don't miss your miracle.

Miracles come in spite of setbacks and disappointments. We need to accept the fact that things may get worse before they get better. Sometimes, a downturn is to be expected *and* accepted, because God could be behind it all. I know that this statement smacks hard against the faith-preaching we often hear today in certain Christian circles. But Jesus said, "[God] sends rain on the righteous and the unrighteous" (Matt. 5:45, *NIV*). Tough times will happen to all of us. Being a Christian does not exempt us from the painful things in life.

There is a misconception that the only time people experience tough times is when they are disobeying God. That's not true. Look at Joseph. He was victimized by his brothers simply because he had a dream from God and was his father's favorite son. When we're going through difficulties, we shouldn't automatically assume that we are out of the will of God. A "no" from God does not always mean what we think.

And God Said No

I asked God to take away my pride.
And God said, "No.
It is not for me to take away,
but for you to give it up."

I asked God to grant me patience.
And God said, "No.
Patience is a by-product of tribulations,
it isn't granted; it is earned."

I asked God to give me happiness.
And God said, "No.
I give you blessings,
Happiness is up to you."

I asked God to spare me suffering.
And God said, "No.
Suffering draws you apart from worldly cares
and brings you closer to me."

I asked God to make my spirit grow.
And God said, "No.
You must grow on your own,
but I will prune you to make you fruitful."

I asked for all things that I might enjoy life.
And God said, "No.
I will give you life so that you may enjoy all things."

I asked God to help me love others
as much as He loves me.
And God said, "Ah . . .
finally, you understand."[2]

Remember that while you're waiting for God, there's significant work to be done in the lives of people around you. But your resurrection day *is* coming. God wants to change your expectations about the future so that you don't miss your miracle. You must keep looking for the miraculous to happen—keep looking for God's resurrection power. But don't expect things to happen in an instant. Instead, expect them to happen in God's timing. This journey is about building a life of faith. The faith-life happens moment by moment as you choose to consistently look for God's sustaining grace.

FOCUS ON FRIENDSHIP WITH CHRIST

Our relationship with God will have a bright future if we do what Mary and Martha did when their brother Lazarus became ill: "The sisters sent to [Jesus], saying, 'Lord, behold, he whom You love is sick'" (John 11: 3, *NKJV*). Jesus is the very best friend that we could ever have. He's caring, trustworthy and consistent. And sometimes, a deeply committed relationship is forged with Him in the crucible of a divine delay.

As we wait for God, we sometimes turn to temporal valves in order to vent our fears and frustrations, when all along God wants to be the One to whom we run in times of distress. However, as we learn to lean on our friendship with God, we will experience a greater level of relationship with Him. When we do, just like Mary and Martha, we will receive comfort and clarity during our time of crisis.

DON'T EXPECT THINGS TO HAPPEN IN AN INSTANT. INSTEAD, EXPECT THEM TO HAPPEN IN GOD'S TIMING.

The first person we call in an emergency is usually the one who is the closest to us. However, if we are not accustomed to sharing difficult things in our life with that individual, we'll certainly not go to that person when we're desperate. Mary and Martha's first response indicates that they were used to talking with Jesus in times of crisis. This is why their friendship with God had a future. They continued to go to Him in the tough times and the in-between times.

God's desire is for our close and intimate relationship with Him to continually flourish, and not fail. He wants us to automatically rely on His friendship during every delay in life. He wants us to know that we can trust Him. We can trust His timing. After all, what is friendship without trust?

For many years, I waited for God, but I was dissatisfied with my level of friendship with Him. I knew that He loved me and that He was always there when I needed Him, but I wanted to know Him better and sense Him deeper. Most of us want to experience God as our very best friend, but we aren't sure how to get there. Yet in John 15:14-15, Jesus gives us a clue about how to do it: "You are my friends when you do the things I command you. I'm no longer calling you servants because servants don't understand what their master is thinking and planning. No, I've named you friends because I've let you in on everything I've heard from the Father." I've learned that the best way to qualify for friendship with God comes by doing what He commands and by trusting His plans.

Focusing on friendship with God also involves going to Him first for our needs before going to anyone else. This doesn't mean that we avoid asking others for assistance, but that we start out solving problems by praying and trusting in God to guide our heart toward His will.

So why not guarantee the future of your friendship with God by trusting His timetable for the extraordinary and the miraculous? You have nothing to lose and everything to gain. Walking with God and trusting in Him is the most exciting and rewarding of all experiences on Earth. I should add that it is also the most difficult. I don't think I've ever met an exception to this rule. Those who walk closest to God are those who, like Jesus, become acquainted with difficulties. Since God took care of mankind's greatest need at Calvary by giving us Christ, you can be sure that He will take care of everything else that He considers to be important for you.[3]

SURVIVAL SECRETS
Remember

The Picture from the Past: A reversal of tangible reality is possible when Christ is intent on helping us accept His divine nature.

The Practice for the Present: We need to focus on friendship with God. When our single goal is to have a close relationship with Christ, He'll be the one we run to when our world seems to fall apart.

The Promise for the Future: God's Spirit beckons. There are things to do and places to go! The resurrection life we received from God is not a timid, grave-tending life. It's adventurously expectant, greeting God with a childlike, "What's next, Papa?"

Notes
1. Dr. Wesley L. Duewel, *God's Power Is for You* (Grand Rapids, MI: Zondervan Publishing House, 1997). Online version available at http://omsinterna tional.org/prayer/godspower/42.
2. Claudia Minden Weisz, "And God Said No," Ann Landers newspaper column, August/September 1996.
3. Charles Swindoll, *Perfect Trust* (Nashville, TN: Thomas Nelson Publishers, 2000).

A Quick Guide to Fasting

Note: Anyone planning to fast should take reasonable precautions. This spiritual discipline may not be appropriate for some who have severe medical conditions. Always consult your physician before beginning a fast, particularly if you take prescription medication or have a chronic ailment.

While waiting for God, you can enhance your spiritual life through the discipline of fasting and prayer. Fasting has been defined as going without food for a period of time to accomplish an important purpose or goal. It is an outward action that displays an inward sincerity—evidence of the urgency we feel for God's power or intervention. Although fasting is not a requirement for people to attain salvation, Jesus implied that all of His followers should fast as a regular practice for spiritual development (see Matt. 6:16-18).

A successful fast is based on a workable plan. By following these five basic steps, you'll maximize your time with the Lord, and your fast will be significant and prove spiritually gratifying.

Step 1: Establish Your Goal
Begin with the end in mind. What do you expect to accomplish by fasting? What do you want God to do? Are you looking for spiritual refreshing? Do you need direction in making a hard decision? Are you fasting for understanding regarding how to tackle a problem? Do you need God's grace or power for healing? Clearly establish your objective. Also, let the Holy Spirit shed light on what He wants to accomplish in you during your time of fasting. It's a good idea to write down your goals in a

notebook or journal and refer to them often as you pray. By clarifying your objectives, you'll pray more specifically and strategically.

Step 2: Choose the Kind of Fast You'll Undertake
Decide on the length of time to fast—for example, one meal, one day, one week, several weeks, or 40 days. If you have never fasted before, begin by fasting for one meal during a given day or go one complete day without food and then gradually increase the duration of your fasting. Also, decide on the type of fast God wants you to undertake:

- **The Absolute Fast:** In this type of fast, you abstain completely from food and liquids. In the Old Testament, people typically used this kind of fast from sunset to sunset (see Lev. 16:29; 23:32).

- **The Partial Fast:** Here, the focus is on the restriction of your diet instead of abstaining completely from eating. Some biblical examples of people who did this type of fast include Daniel and his friends, who ate only vegetables and drank only water during their time of training in Babylon (see Dan. 1:15). Daniel alone practiced a limited diet for three weeks (see Dan. 10:3).

    Drinking fruit juice will decrease your hunger and provide you with energy. And the taste of the fruit juice will motivate and strengthen you to continue. Preferably, drink freshly squeezed juices. However, if the fruit is an acid blend, dilute it in 50 percent distilled water. Apple, pear, grapefruit, papaya, watermelon, or other fruit juices are good choices. It is best to do your own juicing. Otherwise, purchase juices without added sugar or other additives.

- **The Radical Fast:** In this type of fast, you refrain from both food and water or just food (but not water) for an extended period of time. A radical fast can be harmful to your health and, in most cases, should not exceed three days. Some biblical examples of those who undertook radical fasts include Moses (see Exod. 34:28); Elijah (see 1 Kings 19:8); and Jesus (see Matt. 4:1-11).

Step 3: Prepare Your Heart to Meet with God

As you prepare to fast, make sure you do the following:

- Seek forgiveness and make restitution of those you have offended, and forgive all who have hurt you (see Mark 1:2; Luke 11:4; 17:3-4).

- Pray for God to fill you with His Holy Spirit according to His *command* in Ephesians 5:18 and His *promise* in 1 John 5:14-15.

- Surrender your life fully to Jesus Christ as your Lord and Master; refuse to obey your worldly nature (see Rom. 12:1-2).

- Do not underestimate spiritual opposition. Satan sometimes intensifies the natural battle between body and spirit (see Gal. 5:16-17).

Step 4: Get Ready Physically

Preparing for the changes in your eating habits when you fast will help you to avoid being taken off guard by extreme hunger, fatigue or irritability.

- Eat raw fruits and vegetables several days before starting a fast.

• Eat smaller meals.

• Avoid high-calorie, high-fat and sugary foods.

• Limit your activity, but exercise moderately (if possible).

• Rest as much as you are able.

• Expect temporary mental and emotional discomforts such as impatience, crankiness and anxiety.

Most people experience some discomfort during the first few days of fasting but soon gain a sense of physical and spiritual well-being. If your hunger persists, simply increase your intake of juice or water.

Step 5: Schedule Your Time with God
Fasting (for spiritual purposes) without prayer weakens its effectiveness. Planning ample time to be alone with the Lord is necessary to accomplish the goal of spiritual renewal. Be sensitive to God's leading. Remember that fasting is not to be used to manipulate God. It is a sign of the need to experience God's power or intervention (for yourself or for others). Campus Crusade for Christ uses the following three-part schedule for spending time with God during a fast:

• *Morning*—Begin your day with praise and worship. Read and meditate on God's Word, preferably on your knees. Invite the Holy Spirit to work in you to will and to do according to His good pleasure (see Phil. 2:13). Invite God to use you. Ask Him to show you how to influence your world, your family, your church, your community, your country and beyond. Pray for His vision for your life and for the empowerment to do His will.

• *Noon*—Return to prayer and God's Word. Take a short prayer walk. Spend time in intercessory prayer for your community and your nation's leaders, for the unreached millions in the world, for your family's salvation, or for other special needs.

• *Evening*—Get alone for an unhurried time of "seeking His face." If others are fasting with you, meet together for prayer. Avoid television or any other distraction that may dampen your spiritual focus. When possible, begin and end each day on your knees with your spouse for a brief time of praise and thanksgiving to God. Spend longer periods of time alone in prayer and study of His Word.

Don't be put off if you do not successfully complete your first fast. You may need time (and practice) to build up your spiritual fasting muscles. Your fast may have been too ambitious, or you may need to increase your resolve. Wait a short while and try again. Don't give up. Everything we do depends on God's grace and mercy. Eventually, you'll achieve your goal, and God will honor your faithfulness.

Final Thoughts
Once you have completed your fast, you'll need to begin eating again. However, the way you end or "break" your fast is important. Breaking your fast incorrectly can result in acute indigestion or other serious physical problems. The longer the fast, the more care must be taken in breaking it. The greatest dangers are eating too often and overeating following a fast. During a lengthy fast, your digestive organs will settle into a state of inactivity. It is unwise to suddenly overload them with large amounts of food. These sensitive organs must be trained to gradually

return to normal activity, beginning with very small quantities of food.

- On the first day after your fast, eat foods that can be easily digested, such as fruits and vegetables, or drink juices.

- During the next two days, add a plain baked or boiled potato.

- On the next day, increase your intake to include smaller meals or snacks and steamed vegetables.

- Finally, return to your normal diet.

One of the greatest motivating factors of fasting is in knowing that God is listening to your requests and positioning Himself to respond. At times, we hurt so deeply that we think God is nowhere to be found. But even though we can't see Him, we need to remember that He is everywhere present, all the time. Fasting helps you to humble yourself before God. In turn, He will lift you up to a place of victory. Through your posture of repentance, diligently seeking His face and focusing upon His Word, you'll experience a heightened awareness of His presence (see John 14:21).

Through fasting, the Lord will open your spiritual eyes, and your trust in Him will be strengthened. You'll also begin to feel renewed—mentally, spiritually and physically. And God will give you peace that passes all human understanding, even in the midst of your delay.

What Is God Waiting For?
Questions for Study
and Discussion

Chapter 1—The Wrong Thing at the Right Time

1. I entered into a romantic relationship with Tom because of my own selfish desires, but I never really considered what was best for him. Are your motivations pure concerning the things you're waiting for God to do? Are you taking into account what's fair and best for the people around you?

2. Looking at the whole counsel of Scripture, God's timing for your life is gracious, divinely appointed and beautiful. Think about your view of divine delays. Which of these three perspectives needs strengthening in your life?

3. Throughout life, we form various patterns of responding to delays and disappointments. These patterns accurately reveal deep truths about our desires and character. Take a few moments and reflect on how you usually respond to disappointments and setbacks. Do your responses reveal maturity and a trust in God's will or a reliance on your own agenda?

4. While waiting for God, many people repeatedly make poor decisions because of foolishness, a lack of faith, or presumption. Identify friends, colleagues or family

members who have learned important lessons from their own impatience. Ask them to share their story with you. Find at least one transformational truth from each person's story.

5. Think about the last time you mistakenly believed that your timing was God's timing. What tipped you off to your miscalculation? How did you respond? Were you remorseful, repentant or resentful? What are the fruits of these three responses? What will you do differently in the future?

6. Matthew 22:37-39 teaches that our lives are meant to be a divine expression of God's goals and not our own. When was the last time you took a good look at where you want to be in two years, five years, or ten years? How can you reprioritize your desires to line up with the heart of God?

Chapter 2—Caught in a Heavenly Holding Pattern

1. The phrase "being put on hold" has many negative connotations, but it also allows for some positive things to occur. Take a look at the four benefits of heavenly holding patterns listed in the chapter. Which one would best apply to you at the present time? Name some specific ways in which a holding pattern positions you for future success.

2. Waiting seasons allow time for the hearts of others to be touched by the finger of God. Can you identify three people in your sphere of influence who are coming to a new and positive perspective of you during this time? How are these relationships changing as a result?

3. Think about the people who are closest to you. Have you ever blamed them for where you are today? Have you seriously considered the fact that God may be sovereignly and intricately involved in the delay of your dreams? Ask God to help you release these people from the responsibility of making your life productive and enjoyable.

4. A lack of progress in your personal growth and development can leave you feeling disgusted with life. Explore new ways of appreciating the value of this current season by asking others for positive feedback concerning the place where you live, work or worship. Keep a list of the responses that help you the most.

5. Compare Proverbs 13:12, Psalm 30:5 and Psalm 119:174-175. What is the central message of these passages? How does that message relate to finding a cure for the heartsickness that comes with waiting for God?

Chapter 3—Frantic About the Future

1. Explore the downside of giving in to creative solutions for your delay (see the "Overlook Your Options" section). Take a closer look at how Abraham and Sarah's lives were affected by the presence of Ishmael.

2. In light of the question above, examine how your premature actions might negatively affect your destiny. How God might respond to your actions.

3. Read Habakkuk 3:17-18. What would it take to change your frantic feelings about the future into a joy-filled fearlessness? How might an increased emphasis on the eternal greatness of God lift you to a new level of security in Him?

4. Take a look at Fanny J. Crosby's testimony. In light of our culture's obsession with always wanting more, what are three advantages of being content? How can you incorporate Fanny's attitude toward tragedy into your own life?

5. Intimidation happens because we feel threatened by someone who has more talent, power, knowledge or experience than we do. Yet at times, our fears are unfounded. In what ways do you feel threatened by those around you? Is the threat real or only perceived? How does this emotion hinder you from patiently waiting for God?

6. List three ways that you can pursue the peace of God the next time you face intimidation at work, in your marriage, or in your ministry.

Chapter 4—The Long Shot with a Slingshot

1. Think about the sentence "Like a rock from David's slingshot, God wants to propel you into the lives of people who need your skills, experience and unique touch." How is that sentence demonstrated in the life of King David?

2. Can you envision God propelling you into the hearts and lives of others during this season of waiting? What scenarios come to mind? Do you have the necessary skills, track record and character for the task? In other words, are you prepared for God to propel you forward? If not, which of these three areas needs the most work?

3. Take a look at Psalm 33:18-19. How could an increased reliance on the Lord's faithfulness give you a God's-eye-view of your waiting season? Meditate on how He has come through for you during other bad and/or lean times.

4. Godly confrontation can lead to the restoration of broken relationships. Have you avoided a much-needed confrontation with a friend, a family member or a coworker? How can you apply the threefold prerequisites of healthy confrontation (i.e., self-examination, humility and taking responsibility for your attitude) to the challenges in those relationships?

5. Most people cling to security and don't like to take risks for God during waiting seasons. David took advantage of an opportunity to defend righteousness when others shrank from the challenge. In what ways could you take a strategic risk and stand up for righteousness and God's honor in your community?

Chapter 5—What in the World Is God Waiting For?
1. Read Luke 1:1-25. What adjectives does Luke use to describe Zechariah and Elizabeth? If they were aware of the fact that they were "barren, but blameless," would it have made a difference in how they viewed themselves? Does it make a difference in how you see your waiting-room experience?

2. Jesus modeled a sacrificial lifestyle for us and often served the lost and hurting one person at a time. What can you learn from His example of sacrifice and service?

3. Have you bought into the popular belief that true effectiveness only comes when you teach, sing or pray in front of a large group of people?

4. What are some of the benefits you derive from serving or helping people one person at a time? How does this kind

of personalized service make others feel?

5. What keeps you from selflessly serving others while you wait for God? Are there people in your life who you could apply the three tips for investing found in the "Individual Service Builds a Caring Community" section?

6. Think about the phrase "God works through the typical as well as the unusual." When was the last time you stopped to appreciate God's handiwork in the smallest and most mundane details of your life? Are you missing out on the encouragement that comes from observing God's power on a moment-by-moment basis?

Chapter 6—Staying in Step with God

1. Anna had the luxury of never having to leave the Temple. She spent night and day worshiping and waiting for God. How can you continuously worship God in spite of your hectic schedule? How might this practice affect your overall attitude?

2. Identify the areas in your life where spiritual procrastination has crept in. In what ways is your prayer and devotional life suffering? When was the last time you experienced God's presence in a way that impacted you during personal or corporate worship? Is God calling you to a time of refreshing in order to jumpstart your intimacy with Him?

3. Many of us fail to benefit from the positive transformational impact that struggles can have on our lives. As a result, we often end up crawling around on the ground instead of soaring in the sky like a butterfly. Brainstorm

a dozen ways you could avoid getting stuck in your struggle. How can you press through your cocoon to a new place of spiritual freedom?

4. Which one of the two spiritual disciplines highlighted in this chapter on fasting and prayer yields the most fruit in your life? Increase your commitment to living a lifestyle marked by this practice. Ask a friend to join you in a season of practicing this discipline—seeking God for a breakthrough in your spiritual life.

5. Take a day to examine your heart for the presence of foreign allegiances or affections. Are there any overarching preoccupations and worries?

6. How does the command in Mark 8:34-45 affect how you respond to your foreign allegiances or affections?

Chapter 7—Confirming Your Purpose in a Prison
1. Part of making the most of a divine delay is accepting our role as God's prisoner (see Eph 4:1). In what ways does your lifestyle and attitude reflect this truth? What changes do you need to make so that your prisoner status is more visible to others?

2. God's blessings on our life are tied to our obedience. As you wait for God, what are 10 ways that you could increase your obedience and thereby increase your blessings?

3. Much of what we fear about God's sovereignty stems from a distrust of His heart toward us. How can you overcome this distrust? What biblical examples are there of the sovereignty of God resulting in extraordinary blessings?

4. What might God's lack of activity imply about the true nature of tests and trials in your life?

5. How did Joseph's response to his delay play a part in his promotion?

6. God used Joseph's skills to help others long before He rewarded Joseph for his humility and stellar character. Talk with some of the powerful people in your sphere of influence. Ask them about their goals for the next three to five years. Think about how you can adjust your goals to accommodate or promote their desires and plans. Are you willing to be used by God so that their dreams can be accomplished?

Chapter 8—Making the Most of Your Pain

1. Some of our greatest insights about God's character and nature come during our darkest days. When was the last time your emotional pain yielded a deeper revelation of God? During this season of waiting, how did you come to know Him better? What did Hannah learn about God's character during her delay?

2. Consider how the burden of your heart might bring a larger solution to the burden of God's heart. Have you promised to give God your proverbial Samuel? Are you able to pray like Hannah prayed? If not, why?

3. How would your life become more meaningful if you birthed your dream and then totally relinquished it to God? Would it affect how you pray in the future? Would it help you to become more selfless?

4. Read Psalm 55:17. Why do you think that many people never cry out loudly to God in prayer? What are your reasons for not practicing this kind of prayer on a regular basis? How can you overcome the many obstacles to crying out prayer?

5. If you are miserable, it may be because you've chosen misery over other options. Look at the "Your Pain Can Make You Powerful" section. What are three positive ways to respond to the emotional pain in your life?

Chapter 9—Are We There Yet?

1. Compare Acts 1:6-8 and Psalm 90:1-2. What is the central message of these passages? How does it relate to questions about God's perspective of time? How can you adjust your view of time so that it fits more in line with God's view?

2. In the story about the time management expert, we saw how important the "big rocks" are in life. Look at how you're handling your time during your delay. Are there changes you should make so that you consistently give priority to the most important things in life?

3. My husband's story of how God can change the direction of our destinies gives fresh meaning to the truth that our lives are not our own. What are three lessons you learned from his experience? How might God be challenging you to accept a new direction for your life?

4. Think about the differences between chronos time and kairos time. Do you know what season you're in? Review the checklist in the "Five Signs of a God Season" section. How many of these signs apply to where you are today?

5. When was the last time you noticed yourself clock-watching? How might an increased emphasis on God's assurance of your present usefulness help you to break this bad habit?

Chapter 10—The Future Belongs to God

1. Think about how Jesus responded to Mary and Martha's doubts and fears. Do you have the same kinds of emotions as you look at your seemingly dead dreams? Does the possibility of a resurrection do anything for your faith?

2. In Lazarus' case, things got worse before they got better. In the event of a downturn of events in your life, how can you best prepare your heart to respond in faith and not in fear?

3. Lazarus died because of a divine delay. What are the differences between a loss that is allowed by God and one that is brought on by our own actions? Does God respond differently to each of these situations? Can He redeem any loss?

4. Every miracle starts with a need. If you don't have a need, then you don't need a miracle. How can you increase your appreciation for this season since it as an opportunity for God to work a miracle?

5. Read Zechariah 10:6. Looking at God's promises and your predicament, list three ways you can better trust Him for your future.

WORDS OF HOPE AND HEALING

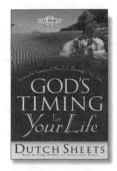

Release the Pain, Embrace the Joy
Help for the Hurting Heart
Michelle McKinney Hammond
ISBN 08307.37227

God's Timing for Your Life
Seeing the Season of Your Life Through God's Eyes
Dutch Sheets
ISBN 08307.27639

God's Now Time for Your Life
Enter into Your Prophetic Destiny
Chuck D. Pierce and Rebecca Wagner Sytsema
ISBN 08307.3834

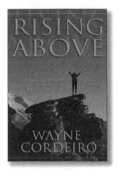

Overcoming Negative Self-Image
Discover Your True Identity in Christ
Neil T. Anderson and Dave Park
ISBN 08307.32535

Rising Above
Living a Life of Excellence No Matter What Life Throws at You
Wayne Cordeiro
ISBN 08307.36328

Hope Resurrected
Let God Renew Your Heart and Revive Your Faith
Dutch Sheets
ISBN 08307.36247